LAURENCE HOUSMAN

THE
ARTIST AND THE CRITIC
SERIES

Volume 1

Photograph of Laurence Housman, from
The Collected Poems, *1937.*

LAURENCE HOUSMAN

by Rodney Engen

CATALPA PRESS LTD.
STROUD, GLOS.
1983

Published 1983 by
Catalpa Press Ltd.

Copyright © *1983 Rodney Engen*

Designed, produced and printed by
B.P. Hawkins Ltd.
4 London Road, Stroud, Glos.

Bound by Braithwaites of Wolverhampton

ISBN 0 904995 04 6

To the Hammonds.

ACKNOWLEDGEMENTS

I wish to thank several individuals and the staffs of the following institutions for their assistance during the writing of this book: Ian Hodgkins for his original research material; Katherine Lyon Mix, who introduced me to Housman's caricatures; Anne Born, who gave encouragement and bibliographical advice; Ruari McLean for his interest and advice.

Much of the preliminary research was guided by Richard Perceval Graves, past editor of the Housman Society Journal and author of the standard biography of A.E.Housman, *A.E.Housman, The Scholar Poet*, 1979. I am extremely grateful to him for advice and particularly for his invaluable biography, which must serve as any author's starting point. Other sources are listed in the Notes section of this present volume. Miss B.E.Barley, Honorary Treasurer of the Housman Society helped with preliminary research; Mrs Pamela Burrough, Librarian of the Street Public Library provided invaluable assistance, photocopies and photographs; and Peter Cormack of the William Morris Gallery, Walthamstow added to my knowledge of Paul Woodroffe.

Those institutions and staff members who helped with manuscript material, prints and drawings include: Robert Wark and Sara S.Hodson of the Huntington Library and Art Gallery; the Tate Gallery photographic department; British Museum Print Room; British Library Manuscript Department and Library. Finally I wish to thank my able editor Shaun Hammond for his dedicated work on the manuscript.

Rodney Engen
London 1983

CONTENTS

I

Heroes in the Garden

"You can't shut out romance from the human heart; you can't shut out wonder. And the romance and the wonder of life will always find in Art the instrument to hand. It may all be illusion, but if it is, so is life." [1]

hen Laurence Housman wrote these words in 1929, he had abandoned a successful and highly influential career as a book designer and illustrator to write plays and novels. But the remark typified his wide-eyed, romantic approach to whatever he created. He was a true romantic with a childish love of fantasy and a poetic gift for turning his remarkably vivid imagination into powerful works of art.

When he died at the age of ninety-four in 1959, he had experienced nearly a century of change; had seen Queen Victoria rise to power and Britain torn by two world wars. He acknowledged these changes, but continued to write with his own romantic view of the world. Eventually his plays appeared alongside Existentialist dramas, his novels competed with the outrageous and the liberated in an age when *Lolita* had begun to shock.

Housman described the first ten years of his life as "the happiest" he had known, because they allowed him freedom to develop his imagination. He learnt to turn his sensitive, private nature into an escapist world filled with the fairies, ghosts, medieval knights and maidens, legendary spirits of nature and classical heroes who kept him entertained and protected from the harsh realities of the world. Later, when he had experienced the second ten years of life,

those "least happy" years struggling to find his voice, he recalled how essential these fantasies were to his struggles. Thereafter, "every decade has, as far as my personal experience is concerned, brought me increasing ease and contentment". [2] It was this magical world of his own creation to which he returned at will. It inspired some of his best fairy illustrations and stories, each one written from a childish delight in his subjects. In later years his sister often heard giggles coming from his study while he worked; "it would be Laurence quite alone, laughing as the words flowed from his pen!" [3]

He was born in the rural isolation of Worcestershire, at his father's ancestral home, Perry Hall, Bromsgrove, on 18 July 1865. He was just one of seven children born to Edward Housman, a local solicitor and his wife, Sarah Jane. As members of a comfortable middle-class household, the five sons and two daughters were highly respected in the quiet country village, where the family's ancestral ties gave them a sense of inner confidence among their neighbours. From infancy Laurence learnt the importance of his secure surroundings, which he added to a growing view of the world. His birthplace, which was not an old house (it was built in 1821), possessed a sense of mystery. Its high gothic windows, flag stone hallways and large rooms, and the fact it was shrouded in a heavy covering of ivy made Perry Hall a house of contrasts.

When claustrophobia set in, there was the chance of escape to the large garden, with its lawn, flowerbeds, the orchard of flowering cherry trees, and beyond it the fruit and vegetable garden.

Favoured among these attractions was the "rubbish garden" of apple and damson trees. Here Laurence learnt to compete with his precocious and ambitious brothers and sisters. Here too they were allowed, to explore undisturbed the two acre plot, "beautifully screened from house", which nurtured their own private, secretive view of the world. In later years Laurence recalled with relish how it was a "protector of our liberties and a field for individual development ... two acres of freedom from supervision for three of four hours daily". He turned the memory into a story, peopled by the god of the garden who understood but never scolded them: "Our Garden-God was a very enjoyable God, but a God whom morals did not concern: and under his guidance we did things which were not wicked, only 'naughty' – that is to say, natural." Here too they fell under the domination of their elder brother, Alfred, who taught them to throw a boomerang or to use his various weapons of war. Each one was invented and delightfully named by him, like the Martin Luther ("a species of gatling gun which never gatled"), or the Flying Torpedo (a stump of wood for throwing), "But if they failed to do much execution, the names made us happy," Laurence recalled, "for Alfred was always able to make us believe that his word-inventions had a meaning, and that the meaning was good."[4]

But while Alfred was attracted to weapons of war, young Laurence sought more placid attractions in the field, and learnt to love the beauty around him. From an early age he developed a myopic view of the world and preferred to concentrate on detail, rather than the sweep of a landscape, or the loftiness of Perry Hall's rooms. He explored the house filled with family heirlooms; its Tudor and Queen Anne furniture, heavy and dark, was eventually banished to the attic and replaced by the intricate carved and ornate upholstery designs of the more fashionable furniture from the Great Exhibition. Here Laurence would freely explore, with his fingers tracing each new pattern in their polished and turned wood surfaces, searching out shadows or the occasional bursts of sunlight that pierced the arched windows. "Beauty, indeed — or what I took to be beauty — was already becoming one of my daily and most lively interests, though the things which I admired were mostly indifferent bad," he recalled. "It began with patterns — the patterns of wall-papers, of carpets, of costumes, of glass, of chandeliers: everything in my home which was there as ornament, I accepted as beautiful without question." His earliest memory of such delight came at the age of two, when he was given a small box with two wax dolls lying inside on a bed of gold tissue - paper flowers and silver leaves. They dazzled him and appealed to his love of detail, which led to further sensations: "Was it then that the doubtful art (which took twenty-five years to eradicate) was born in me? I know now that, for the next twelve years at least, nearly every ornament and picture that I sincerely admired was not at all what it should be. In the church stained-glass windows, mostly rank bad, in the drawing-room florid Victorian ornaments, heavy Victorian furniture, and gaudy gas-oliers; in the nursery, carpet, wall-paper, and pictures all ranged from indifferent to something much worse; and yet, from association though their artistic merit has departed, I love them still," he concluded in his autobiography.[5]

Daily family prayers and frequent church-going taught Laurence about religion. He learnt that beyond the tedium of forced silences and lofty-sounding words lay a new and appealing sense of mystery. His mother had retained the religious beliefs she had learnt during her early life as a local rector's daughter, and taught her children to pray, insisting all the family should gather, with the servants, for morning and evening prayers. Although far from puritanical or prim, she instilled in Laurence a deep respect for the mystical power of religion. Later this would inspire some of his best stories and illustrations, and turn him into a deeply religious, although rather unorthodox disciple of the faith. Those frequent visits to the village church, where the Housmans sat in their own pew in the front row, as befit their station, were a source of new-found inspiration to young Laurence. "I was becoming the religious one of the family — which does not mean that I was becoming good: far from it! But a love for ritualistic observance had got hold of me."[6]

His first experience of politics came from his father, Edward Housman, a delightful man, whom his children adored for his frivolous, often outrageous behaviour. He was also a respected member of the village, where he served as the local solicitor and county tax accountant, although he longed to live as "a prosperous country gentleman", which he felt was his birthright. Unfortunately he lacked the means or the ambition to achieve it, despite his ancestral connections and the wealthy relatives with whom he eventually fell out. In the end Edward remained a frustrated eccentric and dreamy, ultimately tragic figure.

During his early years as a father, Edward was a delightful foil to his wife's religious nature. He could be outrageous: he loved to tell his children how he was a staunch Tory, born "in the year of England's greatest disaster – the Reform Bill". On those evenings when he allowed the elder children to rejoin their parents before bedtime, he gave them a sip of wine and led in the family toast: "Up with the Tories, down with the Radicals!" Edward loved his children, and refused to punish them until they reached seven or eight, and then only mildly. He shared their pleasures, would raid the fruit cages and return to the house yelling "Grubs, grubs, grubs" – his sign for the children to come and collect his latest treat. Or he would pull their toes as he descended the stairs in the morning and giggle as they tried to pull their dangling legs from his reach. On quiet evenings he would read to the elder ones from his latest issue of *The Graphic*. This newly established weekly paper, illustrated with wood engravings of current events and social upheaval "drawn on the spot" by Special Artist-Reporters, was a

family favourite. It taught Laurence about a world outside his rural solitude, where wars were fought and cities were filled with crowds of discontented poor.

But the blissful country life of the Housman family was shattered when, in the autumn of 1869, it was discovered that Sarah Jane had contracted a fatal illness. Confined to her bed, she took great comfort in the Church of England doctrines and even shocked her family by turning longingly to the Roman Catholic rituals of the local catholic community. As she grew weaker, the disease, diagnosed as breast cancer, took its toll and she turned to her children for comfort. Edward faced the news that he would eventually lose his wife by taking to drink. He became moody and introspective; and he spent long periods away from the house and his family. It was a habit he would continue, with greater intensity, until his death. As a result, the brunt of the nursing responsibilities fell on the eldest son, Alfred, and his sister Clemence. Both took turns at their mother's bedside, while ten year old Clemence was equally intent on managing the house and servants, and her younger brothers and sisters as well.

Laurence, who was then five, adored his mother, and now turned to his sister for comfort. Clemence nursed him as well, since at the time he had been forced into bed with a long illness which left him weak and his legs especially limp. It was this which worried their mother until the day she died. On 26 March 1871, shortly before her death, she called Clemence to her bedside and made her promise to take care of "little Laurence. His legs are weak and he will need you." She died soon afterwards, but Clemence never forgot her promise. And although she and Alfred never recovered from the emotional shock of watching their mother die, she accepted Laurence as her responsibility and honoured her pledge for the rest of her life.[7]

Laurence was a deeply sensitive, impressionable child with a seemingly insatiable appetite for affection: "In those days, I loved all my elders with a childish devotion — even their feet were beautiful to me." This was a characteristic, if somewhat bizarre remark. But his craving for love had been seriously shattered by the death of his mother. Like his brother and sister he had been taught to hide his strongest emotions, so that hearing of his mother's death, he fled to the safety of his own room to cry alone. At night he prayed as she had taught him, and firmly believed that if he prayed hard enough and was faithful, she would be restored to him.

Some of this lost affection was restored to him by the arrival of a new woman in the Housman household. She was Lucy Housman, Edwards cousin, who once had called on the mourning family. A rather plain, at times too earnest woman of fifty, with a firm yet endearing frankness, she captivated young Laurence from the start. He was never shy with strangers, and on that first visit, after a quick assessment, he took Lucy on a walk to show her his favourite views and was thrilled to learn she shared his delight in the countryside. She must have sensed his hunger for affection; but she was surprised by the form it took when Laurence proposed marriage to her. To make the offer more attractive, he explained he had £5 in savings and showed her a small cottage which he proposed would be where they might spend their early wedded days. Lucy was touched and tactful in her refusal, for she had not yet told Laurence or the rest of the family that she was in fact secretly engaged to their father. When she returned to Perry Hall for the second time, it was as Mrs Edward Housman. Laurence was embarrassed at first but he long remembered how his father gave him an amused smile, "a roguish look, which meant, I suppose, 'Cut you out, my boy!'" And Lucy soon became the children's "Mamma" and provided the stability so essential to their growing up. She preached her stern, puritanical ideas, filled the house with Lutheran doctrines and brought a new class-consciousness to their lives and the children soon called her "Mater". But Laurence remained devoted to his step-mother who called him her "favourite".[8]

Edward's dreamy escape from responsibility during his first wife's illness had left the family in severe financial difficulties.

Memories of boyhood explorations of farmhouse outbuildings helped Laurence with his first illustrated book, Jump to Glory Jane, *1892.*

Now, with a new wife, he decided they would have to move from Perry Hall, which he leased, keeping only part for an office. He took his family and new bride to to his own childhood home, Fockbury House, in the more peaceful and isolated parish of Catshill, a mile and a half away. The house had been recently vacated, and despite obvious inconveniences like no gas, water taps or main drainage, it was more suitable for a growing family. Surrounded by fields and farms, it was "a good place for children", according to one sister. It was also a picturesque structure with parts dating from the seventeenth century, a half-timbered and gabled upper story and lower plain brick walls. The locals called it the Clock House, since one of the gables had once held a large clock to direct the neighbourhood.

This new home, with its surrounding countryside, opened seven year old Laurence's eyes to a greater sense of freedom. Here were rolling fields, hilly slopes and narrow lanes down which he often walked in search of plants or animals. He and Alfred met their farmer neighbours who entertained them with stories and local legends. They discovered beyond their large garden a world of secretive barns, hay ricks and dark musty out-buildings, and the nearby Lickey Hills to the northeast, with their woods, shrubs and unexpected pools that remain so much a feature of the Worcestershire countryside. Laurence especially loved walks through these nearby woods. Much of that early sense of discovery in nature he later incorporated into fairy stories and drawings of strange mythological creatures lying in wait in some familiar dark, misty forest, or along-

An early passion for fairy-tales helped Laurence fill his drawings with crowds of familiar characters, as in "The Wooing of the Maze", from his own collection, A Farm in Fairyland, *1894.*

Alfred and Laurence on a country ramble, which suggested Laurence's illustration "The Passionate Puppets", in The Field of Clover, *1898.*

side a shimmering reflective pool or under an ancient tree.

He learnt to read with the help of his favourite storybook, a heroic adventure story told with coloured pictures. He tried to visualise his own place in the story, adopted the hero as his best friend, and even incorporated this new friend into his evening prayers. He was devoted to this evening ritual, the mumbled "Cargo bress my dear father, mother, brothers and sisters" which was his infantile way of saying "Pray God Bless..." Such stories played a growing place in his view of the world, and he was delighted when he discovered some new similarity to a character or a storybook place in his widening world. But the border between fantasy and

A princess with long curls held an early fascination for Laurence, as in his "The Traveller's Shoes", from his book, The House of Joy, *1895.*

innocence and became her "favourite" as well.[9]

The more he explored with his brothers, the greater was the desire for freedom. He became more assertive, and often got into trouble with his parents for minor acts of boyish independence. It was as if he felt a greater need to see beyond the idyllic countryside. It forced him to rely upon initiative and invention, as one shrewd observer noted, "Narrow origins, confined within Worcestershire, may have circumscribed his outlook; he was perhaps more self-assertive that he would have been had he mixed in youth in a wider circle".[10] Clemence watched him with concern, and tried to temper his outbursts until she became the greatest single influence, apart from Alfred, on his creative development.

When Alfred was enrolled in the local Bromsgrove grammar school as a scholar and day-boy, he took charge over his brothers and sisters. With his critical manner, he was less likely to sympathize

The Housman children under Alfred's gaze, which inspired "Rol's Worship",
Laurence's illustration to Clemence's story, The Were-Wolf, *1896.*

reality soon blurred and he became confused. For example, he loved stories of fairy princesses with long fair hair, waiting to be rescued. He discovered such long-haired women actually existed when his Aunt Mary came to visit and he stumbled into her room as she was combing her own long hair. Since Aunt Mary was an austere, rather severe looking woman, who always wore her hair in a tightly plaited style on the top of her head, this new image was a shock to young Laurence. The unexpected flood of silken hair falling down to her waist was the sort of hair he had always associated only with fairy princesses, and he clasped his hands together in amazement and exclaimed, "Oh, Aunt Mary, how beautiful you are!" From that moment onward, he captivated his aunt with his with Laurence's outbursts than to demand that they were channelled into one of his various word games, the family poetry competition, the family theatrical, or the family magazine which all the children helped to produce for relatives and friends. Alfred demanded high standards from his younger brothers and sisters, and his numerous competitions were largely influenced by his own interests. He set them nonsense verses based upon Lewis Carroll or Edward Lear, which began when he provoked them with questions ("Have oysters whiskers as well as beards?"). Or there were word themes based upon nouns like "cucumber", his favourite Gothic architecture, Greek myths; or the names of favourite trees to be set in verse. He encouraged a personal choice so that their favourite selections would never match his own. In the end Alfred's influence on Laurence, and all the Housman children, was considerab'e. They accepted his judgement and criticism without argument, as Clemence recalled. "It would have been almost like fighting against a parent or an uncle to have stood against Alfred at that time as man to man."[11] Laurence learnt to believe in his own creative abilities and treasured those early days spent composing and writing under Alfred's stern gaze. "When I was a small child he *did* persuade me that I had written a sonnet which was really his; and he wrote it as mine in the family album." Under his direction the seven Housman children were "seven against the world. How we loved; how we hated; how we fought, divided, and were reconciled again! How we trained, and educated ourselves; and developed a taste in literature and in writing of it, in which, until years later, our elders had no part, and with which school-hours had little to do."[12]

Their's was a private, secretive world, forbidden to their parents and free from the indignities and embarrassing demands of Lucy and Edward. Laurence recalled with distaste the enforced private prayers, "secretive and surreptitious" mumbling in one's room supervised by their new mother. Then came the even more disturbing family prayers, when for three or four minutes after the breakfast bell, the servants gathered with the family, on bended knees to pray. Such ceremonies were "empty of spirituality", Laurence decided later; they "did us more harm than good". Clemence agreed with him and later, when they shared a house together in London, they firmly refused to pray before meals, "in order to try to cultivate a more thankful spirit than the saying of grace ever produced at home".

Linked with such piety was the guilt brought on by disobedience or their mother's displeasure. Once Lucy overheard the children arguing over one of Alfred's new games: each child was to choose one cloud for his own and explain why they had chosen it. Lucy entered the room aghast, severely scolded them for trying to possess what was, after all, part of "God's heaven", and the game was stopped. Laurence later criticized his mother's "excessive secretiveness" which included the absolute avoidance of lavatorial subjects ("the natural side of things"). This reign of secrecy led to the children's ignorance of sexual matters, and their father seeking vicarious delight in the wall paintings of Pompeii. He in fact bought all eight volumes of the excavation report of Pompeii, in order to study the one volume which concentrated on those wall paintings thought too indecent for public gaze. Moreover, shortly after the Fockbury move, he had all his sons circumsized – itself a severe treatment of the younger boys just out of infancy; even more so to adolescents like Alfred. In fact it led to Alfred's belief in sex as a dirty subject. Laurence recalled with bitterness the repression he suffered as a child, which later surfaced in his campaign for sexual equality; writing in his autobiography how "this excessive secretiveness over the natural side of things helped to produce evasion and untruthfulness on the moral side as well, and that the habit of concealment of things which were not wrong extended to things which were".[13]

On the other hand, the secrecy and private pre-occupations of life at Fockbury House gave the children an opportunity to pursue their verse writing for Alfred. Laurence worked hard to please his brother, writing poems and stories with a strong Bryonic influence. He also started to draw, but his writing was clearly more important. "I think my heart was always more in literature than in what is called 'Art'," he later recalled. "But I was far more secretive at that time over what I wrote, than over what I drew. Anyone might see my drawings, but it was generally only to my sister Clemence that I showed what I wrote, in prose and poetry."[14] Much of his early writing was influenced by the books his mother read to them, such as the narrative poems of Walter Scott, plays of Shakespeare, and a particularly dull two volume life of Martin Luther ("from the German"). Their father chose Dickens to read in the evenings to his children, and much of Laurence's narrative skill can be traced to this source. Edward also tried to interest the children in his own "gentlemanly pursuits"; the shooting, fishing, as well as music, photography, gardening and even firework-making which he still tried to enjoy, despite his meagre income.

When Laurence reached school age, he joined his brothers Alfred and Robert as a day boy at Bromsgrove school. Fortunately he too had been granted a scholarship, since the family could not then afford the fees for three boys at public school. On the whole Laurence proved an able student. His only real problem lay in his extreme sensitivity, which made him easy prey to bullying; and his introspective nature, which led to bouts of anguish. Unfortunately the school's headmaster, Herbert Millington, was not sympathetic to either. A man with handsome features and eager intellect who was said to resemble Mathew Arnold, he maintained a callous disregard for the more sensitive boys. He encouraged the use of insulting nicknames among his sixty or seventy students, so that a grocer's son became "Bacon", a farmer's son "Carthorse". Once Laurence was humiliated by Millington in front of his class when he was told to come to class better dressed. It was a painful public reminder of his family's growing financial distress, but the next day, Laurence secretly dressed himself in his "Sunday Best" and crept out of the house to avoid detection by Lucy. As a day boy he was not required to participate in athletics or games, but encouraged to follow his own interests and develop them to the highest standards. He worked hard at his poetry and during the first term, at Christmas 1876, he won a book prize for poetry recitation.[15] He excelled at English but was poor at Latin and Greek, but then Clemence helped him with his English essays and criticized those he read aloud to her. A resourceful student, Laurence did not let his poor performance in the classics stop him earning much needed pocket money from his fellow students. He earned a shilling for an English translation of the ninth book of the *Odyssey*, done for a classmate; it was a welcomed reward since he recalled he was "totally without pocket money for most of the years I was at school".

And yet it was these same Greek myths which inspired his poems and stories for Alfred and became his favourite subjects. Alfred had taught him to study the classics for his various competitions and Laurence soon began to transpose the mythological characters into his own everyday life. As a ten year old school boy he wrote to Lucy about his favourite character, Hercules, and Theseus and the labyrinth. They appealed to him not just because they were good adventure stories, but because they might relate to experiences he knew. "I want to know if this picture is like the old men you see so often sweeping crossings in London," he asked Lucy.[16] It was typical of his talent to transpose ancient themes and settings into modern dress; an aspect of his most successful later stories.

By this time Laurence had entered what he later termed the "most unhappy" period of his life. The root of the problem lay in the family's now desperate financial condition. The household had been reduced to just one maid and one horse in the stable; the children were dressed in shabby clothes and the house was rarely warm. Although the villagers continued to treat the Housmans as respected members of the community, there were unavoidable signs of their struggles, not the least at school and church. Edward was encouraged only by the news that Alfred had been accepted to study classics at Oxford, and he left Fockbury House for Oxford in October 1877. A short time later the house was sold and the family moved back to Perry Hall. There, no doubt under the shadow of his past failures and Sarah's death, Edward again took to drink and suffered renewed bouts of poor health. In May 1879 he had a stroke, tragically timed within days of Alfred's final Oxford exams. As a result Alfred failed and returned home without his degree; a further blow to his family and the morale of his bed-ridden and severely despondent father.

During these trying times Laurence turned for comfort to Clemence, who shared his creative ambitions and seemed to understand what he was trying to write, now that Alfred was away at University. He briefly escaped the household gripped by his father's recent illness, and spent his first fortnight in London. He arrived in a flurry of excitement, determined "to see as many of the sights as could be got into a fortnight". He found the National Gallery the most inspiring attraction and spent most of his time there in the end. In particular he was "curiously attracted" by a painting with strong religious overtones, "The Spiritual Form of Pitt Guiding Behemoth", painted by William Blake. This was an artist unknown to him at the time, and it surprised him to learn, against his better judgment, that it was such a striking picture. "I saw to my sorrow that he had lived in the eighteenth century; and having at the time a fixed belief that, except in portraiture and landscape, the art of the eighteenth century was all wrong, I turned my back on it, and must even have forgotten his name," he later recalled. But the name stuck in his mind, and two years later, while on another rare visit away from home, this time to his godfather in Birmingham, he re-discovered Blake the painter and learned of his poetry while reading Gilchrist's *Life of Blake*. The discovery proved a turning point in his development as an artist. Blake became his hero; a figure who embraced not only drawing and painting, but poetry as well, just as Laurence believed he then might

do. He only regretted "those two years of possible help and inspiration" had passed and been "so blindly wasted".[17]

This was perhaps a harsh judgment, for the next two years brought more terrible trials for his mother and the children. Laurence later called the time "the Purgatory Period" of their lives. By the Christmas of 1880 money was in such short supply that Lucy sent Laurence out to stop the village carolers because they could not afford the half crown they asked for the church funds. Again it was Clemence, now a thoroughly competent and practical twenty year old, who buoyed her family's spirits and tried to help her father's ailing business. She and her younger sister agreed to learn the intricacies of tax calculations and Clemence proved a quick learner. She was highly intelligent, having inherited her mother's good brain, and even impressed Mr Millington, who was generally opposed to women receiving higher education. He once told her he wished he had her as a pupil in his sixth form. Moreover she had a creative nature which Laurence always considered far superior to his own, and he cherished her encouraging advice and knowledge of literature. One of his lasting childhood memories was of Clemence, a child of nine, puzzling over her lines to a poem about Perseus and Medusa from atop her favourite climbing tree. He remembered the lines, "Her brows were knit in everlasting pain, Hers were the lips that never smiled again", which were "rather magnificent as the unaided composition of a child of nine".

There was also, especially now, a poignancy about those lines. They seemed to summarize the self-sacrificing Clemence as she poured over her father's neglected tax work. Each evening, after helping her mother with the domestic duties in the house, she took up the tax forms and worked well after midnight to complete them. As a result, Laurence recalled with obvious displeasure how his beloved sister willingly submitted to the strain and completed the work with remarkable speed. She became "virtually my father's head clerk and was, for two or three years, the expert who worked out all the income tax calculations for half the county of Worcestershire". It was a familiar trap in his eyes; that of the submissive elder daughter sacrificing her life to her Victorian family living beyond its means, when he knew she had greater talents and a higher calling.[18]

Fortunately Clemence had a practical streak which helped to put her present sacrifices into perspective. Like Laurence, her writing was an important outlet and somehow she managed to continue to write, sporadically, and to correct Laurence's school work, as well as to serve under their father. Moreover in the summer of 1882, she and Laurence entered the local art school together; it was a welcomed chance to escape the household still gripped by financial worry. Lucy was resigned to the fact that her sons Basil, Herbert and Laurence would soon have to be removed from their school, despite their scholarships, for the family could not afford their incidental fees and school clothes. Fortunately Mr Millington called to reassure her this would not be necessary; he would make sure such good pupils were retained at the school.

Now a mere shadow of his former jovial self, Edward had forfeited his family's respect and admiration — but not their affection. He succumbed to bouts of dreamy despair which clouded his judgment. He lived in a world of fantasy, and was plagued by guilt and the need to make some effort to help his family. He threw himself into a number of elaborate schemes to make money: he planned to grow pineapples and camelias commercially; he tried to perfect a process of preserving grapes in water to sell out of season at an enormous profit. He even bought land in Wales where he was convinced gold could be found and mined. Each of these schemes was doomed to fail, and they provided small comfort for his children, now growing up with their own problems and uncertain futures. Alfred, for example, had returned home from Oxford a dejected and broken-hearted student. He was given part-time teaching at his old school when his master was away; but he remained a broody, gloomy presence in the house. Eventually his mother cleared the dining room and ordered a fire (which they could ill afford) where Alfred studied for his Pass degree and eventually the Civil Service examinations

When Laurence entered his final school year, he had already begun to consider his own future. His skills at languages and drawing had won him further prizes in French, drawing and recitation. He had a good speaking voice and enjoyed most of all acting in school plays; he made a very fine Odysseus in a school production of his hero's adventures. The theatre was his great joy, and over the last few years his interest in plays and acting became a passion. He sought out those amateur touring companies which descended on small neighbouring Midland market towns for short seasons of melodramas under canvas, and he escaped to attend as many as he could. This annoyed his mother, who "feared that I might wish to become a play-actor, and from my fourteenth year onward small hindrances were put in the way of my visits to the professional theatre". In fact both parents objected, although they refused to explain why. This especially upset Laurence; it was yet another example of family secrecy which left him feeling constricted – a feeling he would always find distasteful. His theatrical ambitions were still vague, however; "certainly at the time I did not act well enough to have any idea of going upon the stage".[19]

But while his mother irritated him over his theatrical interests, she compensated by spoiling him in smaller ways. Now that her husband sank deeper into his own world, Lucy turned to her children for affection and support. She declared Laurence her "comfort", watched over his health and loved to knit socks for his tender feet. He in turn, admired her solid strength in the face of growing financial worry, her stoic acceptance of the unexpected hardships taken on by marrying Edward. Her devotion to Laurence eventually caused a rift between mother and step-daughter, when Lucy felt her hold over Laurence was threatened by his love for Clemence and this aroused her jealousy.

Support and advice of a more remote

nature came from Alfred. Although generally preoccupied with his own misfortune, those days he was not teaching or preparing for the Civil Service examination, he would offer some brief comment or criticism for his brother to ponder. Once Laurence read his translation of an Ovid poem to Clemence and Alfred overheard; afterward he broke the silence with "Excellent", and Laurence was so overwhelmed he remembered the poem all his life. Such was the continued influence of his elder brother. Then, in December 1881, Alfred left Perry Hall and his troubled family to take up a clerkship in the Patent Office in London, unaware then that he prepared the way for Laurence and Clemence to follow his escape to London two years later.

By now Laurence was quite objective about his capabilities. He especially knew he would never become a scholar like Alfred, although family tradition forced him to take the Higher Oxford and Cambridge local examination, where he was examined by the famous wordsmith Dr Spooner, who passed him but not on academic merits alone. Since the stage was clearly out of the question, he had only his writing and his drawing skills as possible future occupations, and he chose to pursue his drawing first. "As I had always shown an interest in colour and pattern, and was fond of drawing, it was decided – with little enough to show for it – that I had the makings of an artist."[20] He was encouraged in this plan by Clemence, who still accompanied him to the local art school and shared his interest in drawing. During the spring and summer of 1882, Laurence spent his spare moments reading prodigiously, gardening and pondering his future, with only a brief holiday to his godfather, a clergyman in Birmingham. This resulted in his re-discovering William Blake's individualism, and he returned home inspired by Blake's inner sense of purpose, determined to model himself upon his new hero. But to do this properly he knew he would have to follow Alfred's example and escape the narrow country life of his childhood for the opportunities of London. It seemed the only real alternative.

The End of Elfin-Town, *1894*.

Tailpiece from Goblin Market, *1893*.

II

Escape To London

nce Laurence had decided to move to London he still had to face the considerable problem of finding money for his tuition and living expenses. His family had little to spare, and his father had alienated his wealthier relatives so that there was little hope for assistance there. Laurence spent the entire autumn of 1882 frustrated and angry at this apparent impasse. Money, or the lack of it, would become the single most trying obstacle in the years to come; but in the end the lesson of frugality forced on him by his family was perhaps the greatest legacy he could have gained from his parents.

Finally, as if by some miracle, Laurence and his brothers and sisters inherited £200 each from a deceased uncle. Although Alfred eventually turned his inheritance over to his beleaguered father, Laurence felt it was heaven-sent. He realised there was now nothing to stop his move to London, and his parents eventually agreed to his plan; but only if he would take Clemence with him as a companion. Laurence was overjoyed by the idea. At last his beloved sister would be freed from her tax forms and domestic drudgery, "released from the Victorian bonds of home, for the sole reason that it was considered too risky for me to go alone without someone of more stable character to look after me".[1]

It was a bold step for the two inexperienced Housmans, Laurence then just eighteen and Clemence about to turn twenty-two. When they arrived at Paddington Station in November 1883, fortunately Alfred was there to greet them. He now shared lodgings with his Oxford friend Moses Jackson, a short distance away in Bayswater, but he curiously avoided his rooms. Instead he took his sister and brother across London, to a friend's lodging house south of the river, where they stayed for a fortnight. It was part of Alfred's plan to keep his relatives as far away as possible from his own private life in London. Moreover he alarmed the new arrivals with his sharp refusal to see them socially: "I don't want you to come and see me at my lodgings: I shall be out or too busy." Clemence insisted he should visit them, in any case; but Laurence guessed his brother was "anxious to have no intrusion into his private life". Eventually, when Alfred did visit them, he seemed a stranger, more distant and obviously troubled, a "fond memory" of their childhood days. And it was to be nearly two years before his friend Moses Jackson discovered, by chance, that Alfred had a brother and a sister living in London. [2]

Unexpectedly isolated from the one person they knew in London, Laurence and Clemence were forced to adopt to their new life on their own. Together they entered what Laurence later called the "waiting period" of his life; those first ten exhilarating and frustrated years in the city as an art student and young freelance artist. With only a vague sense of direction, he found the initiation into London life especially painful, for he had come "to find out in the course of further study what particular line of art I was made for". On the other hand, he possessed the Housman resilience and an unshakeable optimism, tested but never destroyed by years of struggling to earn his living as an artist. He also knew that if all failed, he could turn to his writing, which he now continued to practise alongside his sketching.

In fact Laurence wrote an article about this time, which displayed his descriptive abilities and how dependent he still was upon his childhood love of detail. The article was called "The Strollers", based upon his visit to one of those strolling theatrical company's productions under a canvas tent he loved. He set the scene with a series of detailed and atmospheric vignettes; the frequent gusts of wind made the oil lamps flare up and swing, "causing a very Rembrandtesque effect...a suggestion of strife between forces of darkness and light — darkness becoming an active *force*, a radiating power...Here the powers of darkness allied with the powers of the air, seemed striving to bring about a general collapse: the shadows bounding along the roof, till they grasped at the tent-pole; the wind carried it in its socket; then as the wind fell, the lamps flared up angrily, and away skipped the shadows to the back corners." He went on to describe the play, a melodrama called "Faith, Hope and Charity", with an "impossible plot", a mixture of Shakespeare and farce which Laurence enjoyed with "unholy delight". It was a confident attempt at descriptive journalism, but Laurence did not feel it was good enough for publication until seven years later, when he dusted it off and it appeared in the prestigious literary magazine, *The Cornhill.* He then regretted his early reticence and lack of confidence in his writing, when "all that time I languished, waiting for my literary career to begin".[3]

Lack of confidence entered his art training as well. During his six years as an art student in London, Laurence waivered and grew easily depressed by his indecision. "I did not get near to having a style of my own," he admitted was at the core of his

problem, and years later he assessed these difficult early years in London: "I think now it was a very risky thing. It took me nearly seven years to find myself, to discover, that is to say, in what direction my individual interest and abilities were to find expression; and for some years the routine–training of the Art schools I attended did nothing to help me, leaving me with the depressed feeling that I should never do anything but pot-boilers."[4] His critics agreed and generally dismissed his student work as unexceptional. "Until out of his teens he did nothing to show more than average talent," one remarked.[5]

After their fortnight in lodgings, Laurence and Clemence chose to remain in south London, and found rooms at 36 Camberwell New Road. Here under the care of a kind landlady, they were able to walk to their art school, the Miller's Lane City and Guilds Art School in South Lambeth. This school was a branch of the noted National Art Training scheme and founded in 1854 to provide artisan training to local inhabitants. Now, thirty years on, the school maintained a high reputation among its rival branch schools. It was under the competent if inspired directorship of John Sparkes, who brought a greater sense of tolerance to teaching methods once intended to train only art teachers, but which he now augmented with lessons in the arts and crafts of wood engraving and industrial design. Sparkes was also director of the mother school at South Kensington and employed William Llewellyn to assist him. Llewellyn was equally competent and later became a famous portrait painter and Royal Academician, bringing his high degree of professionalism to the coursework. The wood engraving course was taught by another South Kensington instructor, Charles Roberts, now one of the period's more competent and prolific professional engravers in the black-line style. He had an office in the city and produced engravings for the *Illustrated London News, The Graphic,* and book illustrations after Luke Fildes' drawings to Dicken's *Edwin Drood,* 1870.

Clemence enrolled in Roberts's engraving course and quickly impressed her instructor with her skill and patience, cutting pencil designs of intricate line on the wood block. She had an inherent talent for such work; her family had always praised her abilities as a seamstress and embroiderer, and she had even mastered the painstaking art of "invisible mending". She was placed in the women's studio, alongside fellow female students whom she befriended and entertained with stories. The women students were kept strictly separate from the men's engraving class, which at the time included young Charles Ricketts and his friend Charles Shannon – two figures destined to become major influences on her brother's career.

Laurence's classes were divided into senior and junior rooms, and he was first admitted to the junior; a "decided advantage" he later decided. It allowed him the privilege of admission as a silent observer to the evening Sketch Club critique sessions, where he could study his senior rivals and form his own opinions of their work. Here he heard Sparkes criticize students such as Ricketts and Shannon (whom he did not meet until a few years later), Leonard Raven Hill, the part-time night student Arthur Rackham, and the future designer-engraver, T. Sturge Moore. There were usually visiting professionals invited by Sparkes to pass their own judgement on the work. Laurence recalled the dutiful but bored presences of these painter-giants of the day, men like the genre and animal painters Frank Dicksee and H.S. Marks, W.F. Yeames and Edmund Gosse. He remembered only Laurence Alma-Tadema, the neo-classical master of painted marble, "took heartily to the job".

To counter such lethargy there was the judgement of the outspoken, sharp-tongued John Sparkes. He was especially unpopular among the more sensitive students, but Laurence remembered him and his influence with affection. "His caustic knifings did us good", for the simple reason that Sparkes "really knew his business, and his quiet biting remarks were greatly enjoyed by all except the recipients". Once an unfortunate and unattractive student presented a terribly realistic self-portrait for Sparkes's comments. He was stunned by the quick judgement: "Yes, horribly like!" and the despairing student turned to Laurence for comfort. "It's more than a man's stomach can stand! he makes your flesh creep with his insults; he makes your blood boil!" Laurence smiled, but he refused to agree. He admired such outspoken honesty; it was reminiscent of his brother Alfred passing merciless judgement on one of his own poems. And in the end he was thankful for having been the brunt of Sparkes's barbed wit on several occasions; "though it was not he who helped me finally to my feet in the choice of method and material, and in deciding to become an illustrator, he did give me a grounding in figure-composition which helped me considerably upon the way".[6]

The basis of his early art lessons lay in the rigorous National Art Training scheme, originated by Henry Cole at South Kensington and propagated by branch schools such as Lambeth, to prepare a new generation of artisan-craftsmen for industry. Students were expected to progress through a series of tedious twenty-three stages in which they copied first geometric figures, plaster casts and eventually three-dimensional objects. This prepared them for the intricacies of commercial design work, their final years spent practising patterns for tiles, carpets, wallpapers and the ornamental bric-a-brac so essential to the middle class homes of Britain at the time. Students were awarded prizes in national competitions, their work judged against fellow branch school students in an effort to perpetuate the scheme throughout Britain. Its critics, among them the influential John Ruskin, believed the soul-destroying tedium of copying were mere exercises in perseverance and did little for creative instincts. Laurence eventually agreed, and though he persisted in his course work, and won occasional prizes, he later declared the training a poor preparation for his future.

It was in the face of such tedium that Laurence decided to rebel. He would always declare the need to find his own individual artistic style, and during his early Lambeth training he indicated in which direction his search might lead him. One day he shocked his fellow students by submitting a wholly experimental drawing

William Blake's influence:
a) Page from Blake's Book of Job, *1825.*

for critique, based upon a careful study of William Blake. "I had just lighted upon Blake; and without any approach to his unity of technique in line and composition, had begun imitating him and one day I brought to the Sketch Club a drawing which set my fellow-students laughing. As Sparkes went round criticising the drawings, my heart went down into my boots, for if my attempt appeared so ridiculous to the rest, what would it seem to him? He left it to the very last (having first passed it by without comment); as he approached it a titter of happy anticipation went round the class. Then came his first words: 'This drawing interests me enormously', and the tittering stopped. He went on to say, quite truly, that I did not yet know how to draw, and that my figures were ludicrously wrong and ugly; but he said other things as well. I saw him asking the secretary whose sketch it was (for our exhibits went in unsigned), and when class was over he came and spoke to me about it, saying 'Blake, I suppose?' From that day he kept a friendly eye on me." This was in fact the first real encouragement for his drawings Laurence received; and it reassured him to look elsewhere in his search for a more individual style than his limited art school

b) Housman's "The Feeding of the Emigrants", from The Field of Clover, *1898, uses Blake's sense of line.*

training could produce.[7]

He continued to experiment while on summer holidays from art school. His first return home to Perry Hall since he and Clemence had moved to London was spent perfecting his art school techniques. One of the key skills to be learnt at Lambeth was the chalk drawing of drapery, originally modelled from plaster casts of Greek and Roman statuary. It was an accepted lesson, even amongst those aspiring entrants to the prestigious Royal Academy schools, who were required to spend months on chalk drawings from classical statuary in the British Museum. On this occasion Laurence went out into the sum-

Study of a Blown Raiment
Chalk on grey paper, 11¼ x 14½"
Street Library

mer sunlight in the family garden, and stretched a piece of cloth to catch the strong breeze. He imagined a figure struggling in the wind, his cloak billowing and forcing him to clutch at the cloth. It remains a powerful chalk study on grey paper. Laurence enjoyed this challenge, and was surprised it came out so well. Later, when he presented it to a friend, he called it "my first and last completed drawing in pastels that I can remember making, before I decided to stick to black-and-white". But it was more than this. It indicated where his skills as a draughtsman might have led him: "If this is a fair example of what I could do as a first attempt, I wish I had gone on with it," he recalled. "It is so much more modern in style than my other work; and I might have secured a larger public, and become more popular, had I gone on with it."[8]

By the end of 1887 Laurence, then just twenty-two, had left Lambeth for more advanced training at the mother school in South Kensington. Here, although the training was essentially the same, the school had, over the years increased the number of artisan trainees at the expense of its teacher training programme. There were more fee-paying students who brought a greater sense of diversity and personal ambition to the school. They paid £4 for day sessions, and classes were held every day except Saturday, divided into morning and evening sessions. Here Laurence remained for at least two more years, continuing the training he later dismissed as "years of dull school-work in which much of my interest got wasted". He made elaborate detailed copies of plaster casts in the Antique Room, and eventually won a book prize in one of the national competitions. Ironically the book was John Ruskin's *Lectures on Art,* written by one of the school's most out-spoken critics.

Later other critics joined in, like *The Studio* critic who had been sent to review one of the national competitions at South Kensington. He found it a disappointing display of national weakness, "barely succeeded in raising an average crop even with the modest limits which enclose the practical field of applied art from the vast dominion of theories and visions". There were overwhelming displays; on this occasion 100,000 works were hung together. But in the end, they represented an air of "hopelessness"; according to *The Studio* critic, himself a veteran of such exhibitions: "How often he has entered the show, with new born hope for the school which was founded to advance design and ennoble the decoration of our industries, that we hoped might elevate the taste of the public, and raise the ideal of manufacture to start vigorous branches in every commercial centre!" As Laurence also discovered, the school mostly failed to encourage creativity. "If you feed students on nature, they will flourish; whether as admirable or reprehensible examples depends upon their individuality; but if you feed them on dead fossilized patterns, who can wonder if little vitality is found in their work?" Laurence decided much of the fault lay with the staff, many of whom were too old to inspire; he was taught by "at least two masters too senile and out of date to be of any use, whom the authorities had not the heart to retire to an old age of penury".[10]

As a result Laurence found he spent more time in the school library than in the classroom. Here he discovered the writings of John Ruskin, a figure he had just missed seeing when Ruskin visited the school one day. But it was the writer's poetic prose, his championing of the Pre-Raphaelites, and most off all his belief in art as a human expression and not a mere by-product of the industrial age, which endeared him to Laurence. He was delighted to find they shared an admiration for William Blake, although in Laurence's eyes Ruskin "did not sufficiently appreciate" Blake's genius. He soon adopted Ruskin as "my spiritual father", and was easily "carried off my feet by the strange beauty of his winged eloquence. Later I came to value chiefly not his writings on art, but his political economy".[11]

He was especially pleased that Ruskin shared his displeasure with South Kensington's attempt at national art training. Some years later Laurence clarified his own views on the subject in his lecture, "National Art Training". Here he explained at the core of any such attempts at a national aesthetic lay the need for works of excellence and permanence. A nation must not merely honour its artists and artisans because they created objects for a changing market place; but because they helped teach the worth of the individual, and their creations "recovered the voice of joy" in the country. [12]

By this time Laurence and Clemence had moved to Kensington, to be nearer his new school. They chose a plain, four-storey terraced house at 61 Marloes Road, down a long side road from the High Street. It was an unimpressive house in a long block, but behind it were the mews and artists' studios that made the area renowned for its artistic inhabitants. They brought with them their Lambeth landlady, who agreed to care for them yet again, to allow Clemence more time to work on the engravings she now did for Roberts, which brought in the only money to run the new household. It was a comfortable if bizarre neighbourhood; for the house faced the local workhouse (now a hospital), which provided them with hours of curious entertainment. Laurence remembered how different it was from his childhood of rural isolation; a "situation which offered us the combined attraction of a good open space for outlook, Sunday night incidents between inmates, returning drunk to their homes, and the police, and the stately funerals with which well-to-do families resumed possession of impossible relatives when death had rendered them innocuous". Their neighbour at No. 1 Marloes Road was the writer Andrew Lang, whose fairy tales qualified him to review Laurence's own stories later. Lang too enjoyed the apparent isolation of Marloes Road, and jokingly described to his frequent visitors how to reach it: "Walk up the Cromwell Road until you drop — and then turn right". [13]

Here Laurence and Clemence planned their future together, entertaining Laurence's art student friends, establishing him as a designer-illustrator, and above all sharing mutual interests in the artistic and political world of late Victorian London. Despite brief holiday visits to Perry Hall, they managed to forget their past trials and concentrate upon the future. This turned Lucy jealous of the hold Clemence seemed to have over Laurence; they were inhabitants of another, more exciting world far from the traumas she still had to face at home with the children. Once the renewed threat of financial disaster at Perry Hall forced Clemence home to help her father at the outset of another new tax year. Laurence was dismayed by the loss of his loving companion, but Clemence again accepted her duty and relented, since "it was found that Clem could not be spared during the extra pressure time of Income Tax work which came annually. My youngest sister's health was breaking down under it; and as my father could not afford to pay a competent clerk's wages, my class-mate had to go", Laurence recalled. Yet again Clemence triumphed over this new obstacle to her own independence, and to Laurence's amazement she managed to complete two or three month's work "in a few weeks", working day and night with her quiet yet firm resolve to return to London and Laurence as soon as possible. [14]

The work she returned to in London centred around her engravings for *The Graphic* and *Ilustrated London News*. These intricate black-line facsimile copies of drawings made on box wood by various illustrators and special artist-reporters, paid only small amounts; but it seemed a regular income and Clemence alternated it with writing stories. In fact she created highly imaginative tales as an outlet for her unique religious devotion: tales inspired by biblical themes and folktales, often with bizarre characters and poetic, vivid descriptions. "The Were-Wolf" for example, was a story which had so entertained her art student colleagues that she published it in the *Atalanta* in 1890.

Clemence was, in every sense, a remarkably capable and talented woman; some consider her the most talented of all the Housmans. With her competence in domestic matters, her understanding nature and compassion in the face of adversity, she was much valued by her family. Unfortunately her creative writing and skilful engraving remained overshadowed

Clemence Housman
Pastel portrait by Adrian Graham,
9½ x 7½"
Street Library

by her more famous brothers Laurence and Alfred. But she persevered with her own artistic ventures, despite the lack of encouragement from critics and editors. Moreover, she was a strikingly handsome woman, who never married but charmed those she met in the course of her many activities. With her dark, luminous eyes (a friend once called her "madonna-like") and a passion for social and political issues, especially the infuriating male-oriented government which inflamed her feminist instincts, she was a willing and entertaining host to Laurence's friends. She was an inveterate smoker when it was considered "forward" for a woman to smoke. She was an outspoken critic and passionate disciple of woman's rights, as well as a deeply religious woman who often influenced her brother's waivering faith.

Together they were members of a fascinating if eccentric household: she was "Uncle Clem" to her nieces and nephews, due to her low-pitched voice; he, with his high-pitched voice, was "Aunt Laurence". And while they struggled together to find a place for Laurence to develop his talent, now that he left art school "in search of his own voice", he could not have succeeded without his beloved "Clem".

III

In Search of a Voice

aurence Housman was prepared to use his art school training to launch himself as an illustrator and book designer; but the prospects for such work were, by the late 1880s, increasingly difficult to find. Competition among aspiring art students in search of a foothold in the illustration and publishing fields was keen; and even when commissions were offered they were usually poorly paid and sporadic; hardly enough on which to earn a living. His fellow student at the Lambeth art school, Arthur Rackham, worked as an insurance clerk during the daytime, and studied art at night. The experience made him an outspoken critic of the injustices in the illustrators profession. He resented the struggles he and his fellow fledgling illustrators had to endure during and after their training. Above all, the danger was to avoid the lure of the easy commission; it was the first step down the perilous road of the hack-illustrator. "The living from art is a poor one — for only a very few is it better. For numbers it is dismal failure — for some perhaps who appeared in youth to be really talented and who started with the utmost enthusiasm," Rackham advised a young art student. "As a profession it is one to which no parent would be justified in putting a son without being able to give him a permanent income as well. The fact that you can earn a little money at it now means very little. The standard of work that ensures a successful career is now technically very high and nothing but years of determined study can equip you for equal competition with the rest in the field."[1]

This was a lesson which Laurence took over ten years to learn. In the process he suffered the uncertainty of income, accepted work which was too demanding for his limited skills, and used up his inheritance. But he was determined to succeed, and whatever work he accepted was done thoroughly, with an earnest desire to achieve success. The lack of money was annoying, but a familiar experience after years of frugality at Perry Hall. Even when Clemence's wood engraving work eventually dried up, Laurence persevered in his search for illustration work to suit his own developing sense of style. It was annoying that Clemence had been left with several engraving commissions done but unpaid by Roberts, when he went bankrupt. But such pressure only increased Laurence's resolve to find as he put it, "his own voice" as an illustrator: and if this failed, as a writer.

His first illustration work was a slight commission, secured for him by Sparkes to revise the Vere Foster and Poynter drawing books used at South Kensington. Laurence dismissed the work as "pot boiling", but it introduced him to drawing for publication and earned him much needed money. It was followed by a frontispiece drawing to George Macdonald's *The Elect Lady,* 1888. Anxious to apply his skills to drawing for the printer, he collaborated with Clemence that year, while on summer holiday at home, and together they produced a souvenir print for the local art school bazaar, Laurence drawing the design which Clemence engraved.[2] In addition he alternated such work with experimental writing. Here again he was inspired by Clemence, who continued to devise her own religious tales. He read her work with envy and admiration, and tried his own hand at "writing things which I had no thought to publish—crude essays on social and religious subjects, about which I had ideas, the outcome of emotion rather than of sober reading and study. On fiction and fairy tale I had hardly begun. There Clemence was well ahead of me."[3]

Much of his early illustration and writing was inspired by the literary and artistic mood of the times; the sense of defiance and experimentation so much a part of what we now call "The Nineties". Although this was a relatively short-lived experience, Laurence soon developed a reputation as a minor figure among the movement's fellow young artists and writers, like Max Beerbohm, Aubrey Beardsley and even Oscar Wilde. His drawings and later his fairy tales appealed to the period's search for beauty among the ecclectic and the aesthetic, in an age when experimentation by the young spawned a seemingly endless stream of new movements in art and literature, from Wilde's "New Urbanity" to the cult of the Celt. Their disciples were young men and women,like Laurence and Clemence, who had escaped the restrictive world of their Victorian parents and come to London to find their own voices. They perfected the "gentle art of astonishing the middle class", according to one observer; and helped to bring a more realistic, social-conscience to the world of art and literature. "Dissatisfied with the long ages of convention and action which arose out of precedent, many set about testing life for themselves. The new man wished to be himself, the new woman threatened to live her own life. The snapping of apron-strings caused consternation in many a decent household, as young men and maidens were suddenly inspired to develop their souls and personalities."[4]

Since Laurence felt more confident with his writing, his early experiments to express himself in words greatly influenced his early illustrations. He felt most inspired by the search for a religious voice; some new belief which might incorporate his childhood experiences with a new-found sense of religious doubt. "I was just going through a healthy reaction from the ortho-doxy of my youth; religion had become for me not so much a possession as an obsess-ion", he admitted. When he emerged from art school in 1888, he had begun a story based upon the universal search for God in all cultures, fascinated by the way in which man selects and deifies his gods. It was a recurrent theme in his later fairy stories; this search for a godhead, the universal panacea in a strange and hostile world. He worked often on this story, which was eventually published as *Gods and their Makers* in 1897, several years after its completion, because he felt the subject too private and personal for publication earlier. Again it was a poorly considered decision for when the book appeared it marked him out as an accomplished, inventive writer and became a pivotal work to his literary career. Critics were upset by the story's flippant tone, unsuitable for such a devout and serious theme, but the *Athenaeum* declared it "carefully and often cleverly written", although certainly not humorous. Similarly the American reviewer in *The Critic* objected to his "crude expressions" which were "the texture of his style"; but this did not overshadow the serious theme of the adventure story. He had adopted the familiar Odyssey device, and began the story with two characters, Peeti and Aystah, about to embark on a raft journey. Along the way they collected various nature gods who begged to accompany them. Laurence introduced the quest in a powerful opening passage; "Into Peeti's soul had come the vision of his god. In the midst of the night-watches, with eyes straining at the shuffling darkness, he had beheld it; and as his mental appetite took its bite of the unknown, the divine form grew in clearness and definition..." Later Laurence explained his fascination with the theme: "I have never been able to lose interest in Man's false gods, and in his age-long quest for one which, though unprovable may yet be true". It was a central issue to "the human race, or even one nation", for if man "could only get right about its God, the rest would follow".[5]

Laurence planned to illustrate the gods in this book, but eventually abandoned the idea and the story appeared without illustrations. Those preliminary sketches that survive indicate where he now applied his drawing skills, to those chalk, charcoal and later pen and ink drawings of imaginary creatures which above all suggest the mood and atmosphere of his stories. They are more atmospheric studies, concerned with shading and effect rather than simply illustrating the text. They are attempts to create the ethereal spirit world of his imagination on paper. The charcoal drawing of Chunta-jumbra ("the high-priest's god, an ugly brute, most foul to look upon, ten times the size of Katchywallah") is a crouching feline creature with webbed feet and long tail; but more than this, it is a study in emaciation and terror. It is an early indication of Laurence's capabilities to combine invention with liberal sprinklings of his childhood loves: the Greek myths, country folk tales and classical legends he had learned as a schoolboy.

The strong religious bias in his early career was aided by a growing rebellious streak, as he grew impatient with himself. He associated church-going with home at Perry Hall, and dismissed it on visits in the summer: "It combined much foolish superstition with a smug adoptation of Christianity to social convention and worldly ends". He outraged Lucy one holiday by openly hinting at his new love of high church ritual, which her stern Lutheran beliefs could not accept. His father, however, viewed this new interest "with secret satisfaction", perhaps seeing an echo of his first wife's searching faith in his son. Laurence in fact flirted with Roman Catholic liturgy, as his mother had done; but in the end he declared it unsatisfying intellectually. Later he would stay in a religious order for a time, and ponder the power of Catholic architecture

while in Paris.[7] The experience proved the turning point in his disappointment with the Catholic church; for "in some of the lovely French churches, the tawdry statues, emblems, and ornaments with which modern Catholicism allows its alters to be desecrated, I began to be glad of my escape: unreasonably glad, perhaps, but I cannot dissociate false art with false worship".[8]

Alfred was indirectly responsible for his brother's first published work, when his Oxford friend Alfred William Pollard (1859–1944) became Laurence's first patron. Pollard worked in the printed books department of the British Museum, and was a sympathetic literary man six years Laurence's senior, whose "widest human sympathies and a sincere churchman" endeared him to Laurence. They shared the search for personal religious fulfilment; Pollard being "deeply religious in a mode peculiarly his own".[9] Pollard was also an amateur book designer, competent antiquarian, anthologist, bibliographer and Shakespearean scholar, whose literary interests led to valuable associations with the publishing world. These he now tried to share with Laurence by introducing him to prospective publisher employers in search of an illustrator, designer. Pollard had proven himself a devoted friend of the Housman family as a whole. He had helped Clemence place her Werewolf story in the *Atalanta*, and was outraged by the £5 fee she received, promising to secure better terms for her future work. Laurence never forgot the debt he owed to Pollard, the first patron "to whom I owed most of my early introductions both to editors and publishers — and not introductions alone; he was a constant help to me in the criticism of my immature beginnings in verse and prose, and also in the loan of books for the bettering of my very haphazard knowledge of English literature, limited till then to the books which we had at home"[10] In return he designed Pollard's book plate, and contributed influential articles on his favourite illustrators to Pollard's own publications, *Bibliographica* and *English Bookman's Library*.

Pollard's first and as it turned out most

influential introduction for Laurence was to Harry Quilter (1851-1907), the prolific and multi–talented critic, writer, editor, landscape painter, now turned publisher. Quilter had a keen eye and a sharp tongue; during his brief period as art critic on *The Times,* 1880–81, he earned the dubious distinction of arousing Whistler's anger, which continued to be aimed at "'arry" until Whistler's death. By the time Laurence met him, Quilter had become "tired of being edited" and had established his own magazine, *The Universal Review.* It was launched with great success in 1888, and promised to be "elaborately illustrated". Filled with the work of Ricketts and Shannon, the more established giants Leighton, Herkomer, Orchardson, Crane and Sandys, there were also stories and articles "by leading authors in England and France". These included Thomas Hardy and Quilter's favourite George Meredith. Unfortunately the paper failed after two years, for lack of money, and the last issue appeared in December 1890.

Following his introduction to Laurence, Quilter accepted several of his full page and vignette drawings to accompany various poems and stories by others; also a few articles written by Laurence himself. (See appendix for list) Of the latter, two proved most influential: the passionate "Blake as an Impressionist", and the haunting myth he also illustrated, "The Green Gaffer". The Blake article firmly placed Laurence alongside fellow champions of Blake, like his beloved Ruskin, Dante Gabriel Rossetti, and other Pre-Raphaelites. He began by insisting Blake had been misrepresented; he was not a madman, or if he was it was only in "the sense in which every true artist is mad in the eyes of his uncle in the city, and every mystic to his more stolid fellow-creatures, whose leading conviction is that two and two make four, and that all else beyond this is hazard or folly". He was clearly lashing out against popular prejudices, the philistine attitudes of a utilitarian society which threatened to crush the creative artist. It was an impassioned plea to reinstate his mentor, an artist who had "two great energies— absolute conviction and absolute courage".

He filled his text with Blake's sinewy line and brush drawings, and concluded Blake was the true impressionist, who "ever drew what he saw as it impressed him".[11] This was the lesson of the creative artist; to be aware of, and to use his inner voice, and never to become a slave to conventional patterns of realism.

"The Green Gaffer" was Laurence's first published story, and it marked a substantial début for his talents of verbal description and visual illustration. Inspired by his childhood explorations of nearby woodlands, he devised the story of the Pan-like Green Gaffer, who haunted a wood "in the deep heart of a Bavarian valley", and so terrified the villagers that they soon forgot the reason why. Sholto arrives, a "Scotch boy – pale as to face, ruddy as to hair—wayfaring in search of health". He charms the villagers and sets off into the forest to find the Gaffer, whom he discovers seated in a clearing, a heavily cloaked, and bearded, monkish figure who teaches Sholto about the powers of Pan. The events of the story are few after the discovery, but the descriptive passages continue to delight. The most memorable line, "Above and behind the village street rises the curved slope of the woods, and the blue smoke of the wood-fires lies upon their dark boughs as the bloom on a grape", enchanted Oscar Wilde, when shown the story by Ricketts. Wilde called it "a strange tale with strange illustrations, and a beautiful sentence", which he promised to steal (it later appears slightly altered in his *Picture of Dorian Gray).*

To enhance the ethereal quality of the story, Laurence drew chalk drawings of the Green Gaffer, his mysterious woodland home, and Sholto's meeting, which were reproduced as full page photoengravings throughout the story. He relied heavily upon the inherent fuzziness of the chalk line, and the depth of his shadows, which became almost too heavy, saved only by a Blakeian sense of firm, yet sinewy outline. He added flecks and swirls of light to heighten the atmosphere and lift the gloom of the woods, or reworked the chalk surfaces which he later freely admitted helped to hide his anatomical inaccuracies.

Fortunately Quilter chose to photoengrave the drawings which preserved the subtlety; but on the whole they were too strong on atmosphere and weak on detail. But this would soon change.

Quilter was a cold, distant, highly critical publisher, whom Laurence nevertheless liked as a "boreal blast of a character, honest in his opinions, and uncompromising in his expression of them". His praise of the Green Gaffer drawings was especially pleasing for Laurence, and led to a second illustration commission of even greater challenges. Like this publisher, Laurence had long admired the work of the novelist

and poet George Meredith, "my favourite among living authors". Quilter had published Meredith's satiric poem, "Jump to Glory Jane" in his *Universal Review* in 1889, and the following year proposed an illustrated book edition. For the drawings he approached the *Punch* artists Linley Sambourne, then Bernard Partridge, but without success. On the strength of the Green Gaffer drawings, he offered the project to Laurence, as he explained in the book's preface: "It occurred to me a short time since that a young artist, called Laurence Housman, who had done some very clever imaginative work for me on the 'Universal', might be able to succeed here. He liked the idea, and did one or two preparatory drawings, and, as I thought, with some success, that I decided to entrust him with the whole poem." Laurence

"The god was running at great speed", *from "The Green Gaffer",* Universal Review, *July 1890.*

completed a frontispiece, seven full-page and 36 text illustrations, which he ran throughout his own handwritten text. The entire designs were again photoengraved to preserve the sharp detail of his ink lines, and Quilter prefaced them with his own frank judgement: "Had there been more time there are several of these smaller drawings which might have been re–drawn and re–engraved advantageously".

The book appeared in the autumn of 1892, in time for the Christmas market. Quilter introduced it with characteristic honesty: "Mr. Housman has been kind enough to work in accordance with my ideas, and is to be held responsible only for the drawings, of which I may be allowed to express the hope that the public will think them as good as I do. They are not perfect by any means, and in many parts are open to serious criticism, but the root of the matter is in them—they have the rare qualities of imagination and sympathy, and from the technical point of view, they show that this artist has only to work to become an admirable designer.

Title design for Jump to Glory Jane, *1892.*

Opening from Jump to Glory Jane, *1892.*

JUMP-TO-
GLORY
JANE

A REVELATION came on Jane,
The widow of a labouring swain:
And first her body trembled sharp,
Then all the woman was a harp
With winds along the strings; she heard,
Though there was neither tone nor word.

1

For

At morn they rose, to see her spring
All going as an engine thing;
And lighter than the gossamer
She led the bobbers following her,
Past old acquaintances, and where
They made the stranger stupid stare.

12   When

Opening from Jump to Glory Jane, *1892.*

Whether the world will let him work quietly—whether he will let himself—are questions, only to be solved in the future which is now chiefly in his own hands to make or mar".[12] Above all the book marked the début of Laurence as a book illustrator.

Although critical opinions were mixed, *The Times* was most encouraging, because he "has discharged his difficult task well" by using "quaint outlines" which "reflect something of the essential sadness of the episode". He used a variety of favourite influences, from Blake's book designs for the handwritten text, Sixties school wood-block illustrators for the firm black outlines, the figures and settings done in a style reminiscent of Rossetti, Houghton, Pinwell and Crane. To these he added his own distinctive touches, exaggerating the perspective and proportions of his figures to give a greater sense of intensity. When the devout Jane leaps above the ground, her feet are encircled in an orb of stippled light; a faint echo of the mystical aspect of Nineties book design. Here too he abandoned the diffuse chalk line in favour of a

firmer outline. It was a sign of greater confidence, working on a subject and for a publisher he admired.

The story of Jumping Jane the bobbing evangelist with "wistful eyes in a touching but bony face" appealed to Laurence's religious obsession. Jane's devout faith sent her "leaping with countenance composed, arms and feet 'like those who hang', leaping in crude expression of the unity of soul and body, making her converts, failing to move the bishop, dying at last, though not ingloriously, by the wayside". George Meredith intended it as a satire; and insisted on a sympathetic artist who "should be warned against giving burlesque attitudes... Jane, though a jumping, is a thoughtful woman. She has discovered that the circulation of the blood is best brought about by a continual exercise, and conduces to happy sensations, which are to her as the being of angels in her frame". The story reminded Laurence of Mrs. Girling, the "Mother" of the Shakers, who "though forgotten now, and her community no longer in existence, must have been a remarkable character; and the faith she inspired in her followers was not only intense but beautiful: she taught them joy". He drew Jane as a gaunt elongated figure dressed in a swirl of carefully shaded drapery, her head wrapped in straw bonnet always raised to the heavens where she received her inspiration. He clearly relished the commission, called it "a great joy", and was especially pleased to receive news from Meredith that "my illustrations had the good fortune to please him".[13] Quilter was also pleased, and he continued to call upon his skills after the book appeared. This same year Laurence provided a cover and tailpiece for Quilter's own *Preferences in Art, Life and Literature.* But it was the *Jump to Glory Jane* drawings alone which established Laurence as an illustrator of promise; according to R.E. Sketchley he "hardly surpassed the spirit" of these drawings.

A large part of the following year was spent immersed in reading and studying the poetry of William Blake for a selection of his work, commissioned by a new publisher, Charles Kegan Paul. Kegan Paul (1828–1902) was yet another influential figure in Laurence's early career, with his own religious preoccupations following his disillusionment with the priesthood, which he left for publishing in London. He and Laurence first met, at the instigation of Pollard, at Kegan Paul's publishing offices in the Charing Cross Road (now above the Garrick Theatre). By then the firm was one of the most adventurous literary publishing houses, whose authors included Thomas Hardy, George Meredith, Robert Louis Stevenson and eventually Alfred Housman (*A Shropshire Lad*). Kegan Paul suggested Laurence might compile a selection from Blake, and the result appeared in the summer of 1893.

It was clear from the book's initial reception that it would be a success. Andrew Lang began his review, "To admire Blake is the mark of a clique", suggesting the vogue for Blake studies was growing. Those select few, like Rossetti, who had championed Blake's linear inventions, those "fair tongues and threads of liquid flame" he used in book illustrations and paintings, with that "Shakespearean sympathy with all forms of life and growth" now reached a larger audience. After studying Blake's

Blake's illustrated poems influenced Housman's style.

Book of Job, Laurence was convinced "that Blake was one of the greatest English artists; for me at any rate"; while his poetry, particularly his "Divine Image" was "the perfect expression of religious humanism in English poetry". He developed these ideas in his introductory essay, and converted Clemence in the process, reading aloud bits of the poems or whispering key passages to her when they were out in public. Moreover, Laurence tried to master the Blake sense of line in a series of pictorial borders and headpieces for the *Pall Mall Gazette.* The most successful was to Rudyard Kipling's "The Last Chanty", published in the June 1893 issue as a swirling mass of figures rising out of the bubbling sea, to encircle his handwritten version of Kipling's verse. The bodies are contorted like lumps of clay or extruded pastry; one piled atop the other to enhance the linear flow. What

Laurence failed to understand was Blake's essential message of detail; that each drawing, however intricate, was a mere collection of intricate symbols, precisely and carefully composed. As Blake declared, "I intreat, then, that the Spectator will attend to the Hands & Feet, to the Linneaments of the Countenances; they are all descriptive of Character, & not a line is drawn without intention, & that most discriminate & particular."[14]

A short time later the enterprising publisher John Lane re-issued Gilchrist's *Life of Blake* in his own bid for a piece of the Blake market. Lane was the publisher most associated with the revival of the decorated book of the Nineties, and together with his partner Elkin Mathews had founded The Bodley Head. Their list included some eighty titles by 1894. They published distinctive well-designed books, noted for the beauty of their presentation as well as their literary content. Many appeared in strictly limited editions, bound in cloth and gilt, printed on Japanese paper, or in large paper editions for the collector's market. The book-buying public quickly associated such tasteful book production with the Bodley Head book, and within a short time Lane had earned a reputation among critics as the publisher of elegant, precious volumes, especially of poetry, which many of his more commercial-minded publishing colleagues had earlier rejected.

At his shop in Vigo Street, and his home in the Albany, off Piccadilly, he gathered around him the young, the talented and the influential of London's new generation of writers and illustrators. His collector's instincts for fine glass, china, silver as well as books and prints trained his eye to seach out the distinctive new talent for his book designs; his passion for poetry brought an overwhelming amount of literary talent to his door. His booklist reads like a history of Nineties literature: he published Oscar Wilde, John Davidson, Francis Thompson, Max Beerbohm, Richard Le Gallienne, Laurence Binyon, Michael Field, Kenneth Graham, Lionel Johnson, Alice Meynell and William Watson. He soon published more poetry alone than any other London publisher. The artists he employed are equally impressive: Charles Ricketts and Charles Shannon, Aubrey Beardsley, Selwyn Image, J. Illingworth Kay, Gleeson White, John Fulleylove, Robert Anning Bell; as well as publishing the early work of William Rothenstein, Wilson Steer, William Strang and C.W. Furse. Together they produced the Bodley Head book, generally an odd-sized volume, bound in distinctive cloth or leather, which appeared alongside the poorly printed and garish embossed bindings of more commercial publishers as "models of artistic publishing" (*Sunday Sun*). His admirers grew as Lane's reputation expanded; he had "managed, by means of limited editions and charming workmanship, to impress book-buyers with the belief that a volume may have an aesthetic and commercial value" (*St James's Gazette*). Such success bred loyalty amongst his artists and authors; he had managed to revive a sense of pride in publishing which led Max Beerbohm to conclude "Little Johnny Lane" was "that poor fly in the amber of modernity".

What Lane lacked in technical expertise he made up for in sheer energy and determination. Fortunately he also employed some of the period's most skilled technicians; designers like W.B. Blaikie of T.A. Constable and Charles Jacobi of the Chiswick Press, who worked with his growing number of artist illustrators. He chose these artists largely on instinct. Once, in response to Frederic Leighton's praises of Aubrey Beardsley's limited talent ("Ah, if he could only draw!"), Lane replied, "Sir Frederic, I am sick of seeing the work of men who 'can only draw!'". This was the spirit in which he now turned to the relatively unknown Laurence Housman. He noticed how Laurence had recently distinguished himself with his publisher colleague Kegan Paul, and asked Laurence to design a trial book. Its success and especially the thoroughness with which he attacked this new prestigious commission, impressed Lane. He quickly became one of Lane's most competent and influential book designers, whose innovations lived on long after he left the privileged employ of the great John Lane.

From the beginning, Laurence shared

Lane's absolute belief in the total unity of a book's design. From binding to typefaces and layout to illustrations, the book must appear as a distinctive whole. This echoed the voices of such pioneers of the revival of fine printing as Emery Walker and William Morris. Walker had in fact set out his book design principles in a lecture as early as 1888 (recently reprinted in *Arts and Crafts Essays*, 1893). He stressed the importance of ornament, "whether picture or pattern-work, should form part of the page, should be part of the whole scheme of the book". He borrowed the aesthetic of fine printing from those early press books with their crude woodcut illustrations and heavy handset type, where "the proportions of the page still give pleasure by the sense of richness that the cuts and letters together convey". In the end, he believed a designer's goal was simple: "Therefore, granted well-designed type, due spacing of the lines and words, and proper position of the page on the paper, all books might at least be comely and well-looking; and if to these good qualities were added really beautiful ornament and pictures, printed books might once again illustrate to the full position of our Society that a work of utility might be also a work of art, if we cared to make it so."

Laurence also began his designs for John Lane under the influence of Lane's most impressive new design discovery, Charles Ricketts, who had himself just turned full-time book designer and illustrator. His early binding designs for Lane remain the essence of the Bodley Head book, from the tall elegant simplicity of willow leaves and fluted line on the cover of Gray's *Silverpoints,* 1893, to the exotic hints of Persian saddle books, Japanese and Greek simplicity of line for the spare binding to Oscar Wilde's *The Sphinx,* 1894. Laurence learnt the essential lesson of simplicity from Rickett's binding designs, and to assimilate those influences which interested him. A Ricketts book was an unmistakable object in its own right; stark, elegant, mathematically precise, softened only by gilt or brightly coloured, embossed lines. Above all, it was a totality; carefully composed so that each part was compatible yet striking; like musical counterpoint in ink and paper.

Ricketts was particulary influential as a designer and illustrator for his own printing press at the Vale, Chelsea, where he and Shannon produced *The Dial*, their own magazine of art and literature. Laurence learnt of the first issue sometime in 1890, and he called on Ricketts at The Vale in search of a copy. This first meeting proved a turning point in Laurence's own attitude towards illustration, for not only did he see where *The Dial* was produced, but he was shown by Ricketts those elaborate ink drawings of medieval subjects he was preparing for process engraving in the *Magazine of Art* and the newly formed *Black and White* magazine. Their dense pen and ink surfaces were so different from Laurence's indistinct chalk drawings; the intricate shading of knights and dense background foliage was done in a technique Ricketts called "filigree", and inspired by "an almost Persian finick and finish". It was a shocking revelation. Here was a total blend of his mentors' styles: Blake's linear rhythms, with Pre-Raphaelite subjects, and the dense tonal surfaces of his admired Sixties School illustrators, often set inside a heavy medieval border. Moreover, *The Dial* reproduced bold woodcuts and experimental engravings which brought an originality to past conventions in printing. In fact Laurence had known of the existence of fine bindings and early printing at an early stage. At the age of eight he and Alfred had discovered the remains of their grandmother's library in a musty attic at Fockbury House. Here the heavy volumes, some dating from Caxton's time, were in a dreadful state, his insensitive grandmother allowing her children to tear up the covers to use as wads in their muzzle-loading guns while she sold the paper pages for butter paper. And now, here in Ricketts's studio were examples of innovation borrowed from those same early typographical models. Laurence recalled the result: "Within a month Ricketts had dragged me away from my timid preference for fuzzy chalk drawing, as a means of concealing my bad draughtsmanship, and had set me to pen-work, with Rossetti and other Pre-

Charles Ricketts's influence: a) Housman's use of Ricketts's filigree ink work in "The Merciful Drought", from All Fellows, *1896.*

b) Woodcut line borrowed from The Dial *for "The Heart of the Sea", used in* All Fellows, *1896.*

Raphaelites as my main guides both in composition and technique. From that time on I felt set — I acquired a new confidence; I had found at last what I wanted to do."

Unfortunately while Laurence always recognized his debt to Ricketts ("that debt must ever remain"), theirs was a short-lived friendship. Laurence found his friend's exuberant, out-spoken manner too over-whelming for his own uncertain sensibilities, especially his early plans to adopt Ricketts's style of pen drawing to his own purposes. His visits to The Vale eventually stopped, because there Ricketts was too demanding; with his "strained and restless brilliance... ever laying down the law with an arbitra-riness which the quick change of some of his admirations did nothing to modify". Even more to the point, Ricketts was amused by Laurence's religious obsession, and clearly upset him by saying he was "dotty about God"; a remark Laurence dismissed later as "unsympathetic criticism". His visits became ordeals, in which he felt himself running "a zigzag course of acceptance and escape". And while he enjoyed Ricketts's partner, Charles Shannon, and regretted giving up exposure to his "quiet blend of modesty and confidence", which were more comfortable virtues echoing his own childhood training, Laurence soon broke with Ricketts and Shannon and they never met again.[16]

But the lessons he learnt at The Vale gave him confidence enough to produce, over the next few years, at least ten successful book design commissions for John Lane. He developed his own outspoken approach to such work, and especially became an influential exponent of the inventive book format, a concept largely ignored by Ricketts. He made it clear from the start that he must have some control over a book's format; it was "as unreason-able to expect a designer always to design within a set format as it would be to expect a painter to paint within a frame of a fixed size and shape". He was credited with inventing, or at least popularizing such book sizes as the tall narrow octavo (*Goblin Market*), the squat, almost square

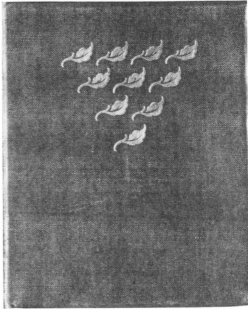

Housman's binding designs for John Lane.

octavo (Thompson's *Poems*) and the slightly higher, narrower octavo (*The Were-Wolf*); the last two previously known only from Victorian shilling toybooks for children and never considered suitable for adult literature. Such formats gave him greater scope for cover and binding decoration. He employed at least three formulas here: the pure pattern overall in an intricate linear tapestry of gilt tracery stamped on plain coloured cloth; the use of figures and elaborate borders linked to the illustrations inside; and the simple geometric shapes in sparse compositions embossed upon bare boards. Inside he favoured a concentration of illustrations, the careful placement of elaborate interlace borders around a title page and frontispiece to unify them; a similar interlace for initial letters drawn to enchance the chosen typeface. The text itself was carefully composed with wide margins and usually set upper-left to give the Ricketts-inspired impression of elegant simplicity. In the end, his book designs echoed Walker's tenet of the totally unified, balanced and well-proportioned whole.[17]

John Lane was meticulous and demanding with his designers. He provided them with a book's exact details of type, paper and binding materials, after consultations with his printers, and in return he expected the designer to not only provide drawings but to superintend their work through the presses, to make arrangements for the supply of all materials and labour for printing, issuing and binding. Unless other arrangements were made at the outset, Lane retained the copyright of all illustrations. Fortunately a few of Laurence's letters to Lane during the period of his early commissions survive. They indicate how seriously he accepted the excessive demands Lane placed upon his new designer, and why his resulting designs remain respected examples of early Nineties commercial printing.

The first commission was for a cover design, title page and frontispiece to Francis Thompson's *Poems.* The poems themselves, the work of the vagabond poet who combined a love of Blake with his own devout Catholic sentiments and Christian mysticism, appealed to Laurence's religious nature. He began work directly after the Blake selections volume appeared, in late summer 1893. By 31 August he completed a second frontispiece illustration based on the poems, having had the first rejected by Lane. Then followed the cover design he specified "printed in solid gold". But the problem of integrating this cover with the intricate pen work of his frontispiece and the spare title page became a stumbling block, and only after two attempts at the title design did he submit the final version which he instructed Lane should "have a good strong type that will give about the same colouring as the design, and, it may be well to set the lines closer together than I have indicated in order to keep the lettering solid and also I think improve the shape of the page". Borrowing a lesson learnt from Ricketts, he suggested these should be printed in an "experimental red ink". Laurence even at this early stage had a sharp eye for printed detail, and insisted on the printer's complete obedience to his preliminary plans: the title page date had to be moved, since the proofs had it "a little too far to the right, please have this corrected", he told Lane, writing "In great haste". Then he added a postscript: "Don't take my lettering of 'POEMS' as a standard. I should prefer something lower and broader. Anything that will take off the height consistent with good lettering will be an improvement."[18]

These exacting negotiations between Laurence, Lane and the printer were generally done by post, and proved as irritating to Lane as to his designer. For example, Lane approved the red ink but Folkard, his printer, failed to get the right colour. Laurence was outraged when he received the proofs not only for the title page but for the frontispiece as well, all printed in red, "which of course was all wrong". He decided Folkard had "a fatal love of pink", for even the colour ink was wrong, and subtlety was the key to the success of his designs. Laurence had in fact considered a rough textured paper for his frontispiece alone, to give the dense

ink drawing (the only illustration in the book), a more substantial and solid impression. "I almost prefer the disadvantage of the rough paper for the frontispiece rather than have a paper noticeably different in colour. A smooth died (sic) surface would be best. I hate a glaze," he told Lane, whom he again warned against his slipshod printer. To be safe, he insisted that Lane must check all stages of the proofs himself: "They do not seem to be accurate copiers of what is set before them in the way of arrangement."[19] Finally, three days after receiving the final frontispiece and title proofs, Laurence approved the work in time for the book to be sent for exhibition at the fourth Arts and Crafts Exhibition in London. His patience and care had finally paid off, and the book was displayed alongside such new productions as Ricketts and Shannon's *Daphnis and Chloe* designs. *The Studio* reproduced his binding design alongside its review of the exhibition, and noted it was just one of several noteworthy book designs by a new generation of artists, whose influences were certain to spread to future generations "to an unusual extent".[20]

True to his meticulous nature, Laurence was still not entirely satisfied with the book, and when he learnt from Lane there was a chance for final revisions, he wrote to ask if the title page could be changed. "I should like the upper set of type to be dropped to within 1/10th of an inch of the top of the design, and for the three lines not to have more that 1/10th inch of leading between them: Poems and Francis not to have more space between them than Francis and Thompson."[21] Later, when a second edition was ordered in December 1893, he again tried to alter his design, changing the title page to rough paper, the frontispiece to smooth. "It would be better", he told Lane.[22]

The book appeared in the shops in November 1893, in time for Christmas sales, and a second edition had to be ordered a month later. The designs enhanced Laurence's reputation as a fledgling book designer, associated him with John Lane's successes, and hardened his own attitude toward professionalism in book design. A

POEMS
BY FRANCIS
THOMPSON

LONDON AND NEW YORK
JOHN LANE, THE BODLEY HEAD
1904

Title to Francis Thompson, Poems, 1893, retained in this later 1904 edition.

---

recent critic called it "in every way a triumph of imaginative book design".[23] It was placed in the shops alongside other Lane publications, but it's distinctive almost square shape, bound in grey paper boards with the triangular design of six embossed gilt circles on the cover, a cluster of similar circles on the spine, set it apart from rival books of poetry. What the public did not know, was that the grey boards were a compromise by Lane, who grew impatient with Laurence's obsessive demands for a "grey brown" colour binding.

Frontispiece to Francis Thompson, Poems, 1893, used symbolic figures.

He discovered this colour while on holiday, how it could by made "by applying shell-lac varnish to the brown papers", and he pestered Lane with variations on this minor subject until Lane gave up and ordered the uniform grey colour for the first edition of 500 copies; later the second edition was bound in green cloth.

Inside too, the book was a surprise to those expecting the conventional designed book of verse. The title page was a stark tribute to medieval printing, an oblong block of type set off-centre and upper left, adrift in the surrounding sea of white margin. Only the small motif of three stylized cone-shaped flowers and tendrils, printed in dullish red brown-ink, relieved the impression of bold simplicity. It was a daring début, especially in contrast to the opposite frontispiece drawing with its intrical jewel-like ink surfaces. It depicted two symbolic figures, one wrapped in a thick cloak, the other with bare back to the viewer; a symbolic tribute to the poems that followed, drawn in a mixture of Rossetti's and Ricketts's styles.

By the end of 1893 in fact, Laurence had completed designs for four books, as well as various drawings for magazines and occasional articles. But even this prolific output failed to provide enough financial security to free his mind of worry. After completing the Thompson designs, he planned to leave London on a month's holiday, visiting friends in the north. Significantly, he announced this plan to John Lane with the added plea, "but if any small piece of design wants doing in a hurry I will try to attend to it". He then clearly needed the money; later he called this trying early period "living (to put it figuratively) with only a pound or two between me and the work-house across the road". Forced to take on as much work as he could manage, he eventually earned about £2 to £3 a week over long periods between 1892 and 1900; or sometimes as little as £50 a year. His first successful year as a freelance brought in £146 13s 6d, but such income was never reliable or regular, even at the best of times. He was probably paid by John Lane on a scale with his fellow designers: Ricketts had

earned five guineas for his first Lane commission (half-title, title page and cover design to *Wilde's Poems*, 1892). It was a difficult lesson to learn, this uncertain darkening financial cloud which hung over him until he was forty-six. Even as late as 1907 he admitted he never had a business sense. Writing to advise an aspiring young woman artist then, he declared how he had "no idea about market prices but his rough notion of the value of an honest artist is £50 a month".[24]

Gradually he became seasoned by the parsimonious habits of publishers. He generally submitted his account with his final drawings for John Lane, who was noted for delaying payment to all his artists. In the early stages of their collaboration, Laurence felt trapped by the typical freelance impasse — he could not afford to alienate his publisher employer by demanding payment; he could not afford to continue to design until he was paid. On such occasions Laurence relied upon his wit, a keen sense of humour, and invaluable tact. Once, after several unsuccessful attempts to prise his £5 fee from Lane, he wrote him a polite letter requesting a £5 loan, which he promised to repay as soon as his publisher, "a most honourable man", paid him that amount promised the previous week. Lane was so amused by this subtle but effective reference to himself, the "honourable" publisher, that he sent the £5 by return of post and later entertained his friends with the story, raising the amount to £50 for effect.[25] Later, seasoned by such humiliations, Laurence accepted Lane's offer to translate a book for him, but only for a staggering £20,000 fee; needless to say the project never materialized. But on the whole, Laurence was grateful for the commissions offered to him, and noted in his autobiography, with the benefit of hindsight, "I have met instances both of stinginess and sharp-practise, they have been the exception, and not the rule".[26]

Spurred on by financial worry, Laurence could not afford his holiday, and worked on the next Lane commission throughout his month's escape from London. With the benefit of the Thompson *Poems* experience, he completed the cover design, frontispiece and title page to John Davidson's *A Random Itinerary* much quicker, and the book in fact appeared some sixteen days after the Thompson *Poems* was published. He completed the frontispiece ink drawing at Banbury, and received the printer's "rotten" proofs at Alnwick. There he paused to write a typical outraged reply to Lane, about the "miserable printer" who could not "set up his type by the copy which is set before him, instead of vexing the soul of an unhappy artist away for his holiday".[27]

The book itself offered new challenges. John Davidson, the austere Scottish author who had written this prose record of his favourite walks within ten miles of Charing Cross originally for magazine publication, was difficult to please. When Lane proposed a book edition he was well aware of the author's outspoken distaste

———————————

Frontispiece and title design for John Davidson, A Random Itinerary, *1894.*

for "fanciful" book design; he insisted all his works should appear in "plain, honest dark blue buckram", and Lane had to agree. Laurence, however, had other ideas, which on the whole were accepted. For example, the frontispiece of a weary family group shrouded in shadowy despair, reflected Sixties school wood engravings. Again he made the title page into a block set upper left and off centre, with a simple but effective abstract design of coils or snail shells ("art nouveau curls of hair" according to one critic). Although the general impression was less ordered and precise than the Thompson book, Lane was pleased enough with the title page motif to re-use it later (upside-down) for Monkhouse's *Books and Plays*, 1894. The binding also troubled Laurence, and he planned a "dress material" which he sent as a sample for Lane's approval, on which the cover design was to be gilt-stamped. It is not known whether the final published binding, a rust-coloured coarse grain linen, was Laurence's choice; but it must certainly have pleased the austere taste of the book's author.

A RANDOM
ITINERARY

By JOHN
DAVIDSON

LONDON
ELKIN MATHEWS
AND JOHN LANE
BOSTON
COPELAND & DAY   1894

Through his frontispiece drawings for John Lane, and various magazine illustrations, Laurence discovered the art of illustration was an exacting and demanding profession. It demanded a thorough reading of the text before subjects and compositions could be proposed, and under Lane's censorship, he learnt to seek clarity and abandoned his preoccupation with more obscure symbols. Lane was indeed strict with him; he refused to accept frontispiece designs he felt too obscure, or even obscene. In the end, Laurence became an outspoken champion of the art of book illustration, and wrote several influential articles which helped to revive the influence of artists he felt had succeeded but were now neglected. They taught the present generation of illustrators about the merits of artists like Arthur Boyd Houghton, Arthur Hughes or the Pre-Raphaelites. Like his contemporary Beardsley, he approached illustration first as a decorator concerned with evoking a distinctive style, usually filled with intricate pen work detail and rich surface shading. Above all, he believed the true illustrator must have a distinctive style and retain his own individuality; not just "take up the text of a book and accurately convert any plain statements it may contain into a picture", for that was merely cataloguing of things already known". The true illustration "becomes not what we so often find, the dull repetition, through another medium of things already sufficiently made clear by the text; but something new with further appeals and fresh charms for the imagination... in a word, the result of another creative faculty at work on the same theme". [28]

The roots of this theory came from his own experimentation: drawing in chalk, pencil or pen and ink for wood engraving and process techniques, adopting his art school lessons of drawing within a set framework (for example the tedious tile design lessons set to fill geometric shapes). From 1890 onward, Laurence discovered how much could be learnt from book-plate designs as well. He created at least fourteen different book-plate designs for various friends and patrons (see appendix). One of the earliest and most successful was done for A.W. Pollard in 1890, and depicts a simple winged scholar figure encircled by heavy strapwork. *The Studio* critic and editor, Gleeson White, called it "a most ingenious plate". Most of these book plate designs were drawn for wood engraving, although one, Robert and Evelyn Benson's roundel filled with a masted ship, was probably planned for process engraving. It shows the care Laurence took over even the smallest designs (here just 65mm across), and exists in at least three versions: one with a lamp at the ship's stern to illuminate and enhance his intricate shading; a second drawn in weaker line, probably for process engraving; and a third version without the lamp and framed by an additional heavy outer border. [29]

It was this Benson book plate which introduced Laurence as a book plate

Housman's book plate for Robert and Evelyn Benson, 1890.

designer to a larger public. Norna Labouchère listed it in her pioneering *Ladies Book Plates*, 1896; as did Henry Fincham in his influential *Artists and Engravers of British and American Book Plates*, 1897. The following year Gleeson White announced Housman was a major designer of Ex Libris, and reproduced a late example of his inventiveness: "Ex Libris Huberti Bland", the splendidly

Book plates by Housman.

elegant figure of a knight in full armour holding a giant sword, a swirling peacock feather in his helmet, his chain mail and rippling armour masterfully detailed and engraved. "Why more people do not endeavour to secure designs by Mr Housman (cut on wood, if possible, by his sister) is a mystery. Perhaps he declines commissions, for there seems no other logical reason for that most ingenious and accomplished draughtsman being represented by such a small number of book-plates which his art would at once raise to something worth possessing, worth treasuring," Gleeson White concluded.[30]

From a careful study of the Sixties School illustrators, Laurence believed he and his fellow illustrators could bring to their work a new freshness, and lighten up the oppressive heaviness of book designs still suffering under "the terrible shadow of the Great Exhibition...[which] spawned the heavy, ornate book covers and decorations, ill-conceived and poorly printed that typified the period of the 1850's". The legacy of these past designers brought mixed blessings which he wanted to help sort out; "if it did nothing more, it bred in the English public a sincere craving for what was elaborately and barbarously bad in art. Popular editions sprang to meet the demand, and books, in covers that remind one sometimes of casket-work, sometimes of confectionary, or, in extreme cases, of the Albert Memorial, and inwardly adorned with borders of rustic porches, Oxford frames, and Owen Jones ornament, epitomised for thousands of harmless readers the vices of a state-fostered art revival." Laurence urged young artists to search out the most effective examples, "submerged in popular editions whose binding, and 'decorative' borders combine to rob it of its effect and obscure the apparentness of its aim". He included illustrators like Rossetti, Houghton, Hughes, Pinwell, Walker, who had brought some originality to the "chaos of bad art and cheerful depravity" with their drawings "full of instinct for decorative fitness"; they were creators of "beauty and distinction amid the sordid conventions of common-place".[31]

Laurence's own attempts to borrow from his revered Sixties School mentors led to drawings of greater intricacy, his surfaces carefully built up into pools of light and shadow reminiscent of Rembrandt's mastery of light and darkness. Since many were prepared for wood engraving, he sought advice from Clemence as to which passages would retain their clarity, once the graver had transformed them into fine line upon the wood block. He studied the expert technique of Arthur Boyd Houghton, who had produced such marvels of gesture and detail for *Good Words* and *The Graphic*, all expertly wood engraved by the Dalziel Brothers. Laurence especially admired Houghton's naturalism; he was a draughtsman who had "shown how far style may reach into realism, giving squalor, ugliness, even vulgarity, and yet retain its distinctive tone throughout". Later he published a selection of Houghton's best drawings and urged his readers to study their engraved detail: "For texture, or the mould of a limb, for all intricate blendings of form, for the qualities of atmosphere and sunlight, his eye had all the keenness of a realist's. For flow of line, disposition of mass or balance of tone, he was a stylist and designer, working in decorative values to a decorative effect."[32]

Much of this concern for engraved detail appeared in the growing number of book illustration commissions he completed over the next five years. The first significant exercise was the twelve full page drawings he made to accompany a selection of Danish folk tales by Jonas Lie, translated for the first time into English by R. Nisbet Bain. Laurence dismissed the venture later as "no particular value", but at the time it gave him an opportunity to stretch his powers of interpretation and **create some imaginative and striking, if** uneven images, despite the fact the drawings had to be sandwiched in between his Lane commissions. Published by Kegan Paul as *Weird Tales From Northern Seas*, in November 1893, the eleven folk tales of Scandinavian fishermen dogged by the powers of Nature, were particularly appealing subjects. They were filled with weird supernatural events and haunting spirits, like the phantom Dravg, a malignant

a)

b)

c)

d)

demon who sailed the sea in a half boat which could only be seen by men on the edge of death; or the Gan-Fin, a totally evil spirit who sold renegade winds by the sackful and sent raging winds and violent storms or dense fogs to those fishermen who offended him, aided by his army of relentless messengers, the gan-flies, who were capable of scattering fatal diseases on the winds. It was generally a rather gloomy collection, full of nordic doom and hopelessness. But their author, Jonas Lie, had recently undergone something of a revival, especially in America, and Kegan Paul hoped to monopolize on this new market.

Much of his hope for the book rested upon the illustrations, which had to be descriptive, yet intriguing enough to capture the book-buying public. Laurence rightly concentrated upon atmosphere in the tales. He took a lesson from Houghton and emphasized essential details: the twist of a frightened body, the gaping mouth of a terror-struck victim with eyes widened in horror at the sight of some new sea demon. He succeeded best when he concentrated upon sharp outline: placed a tortured figure against a stark white background, or picked out a face enveloped in dark shadow, borrowing Houghton's trick of using flecks of white to accentuate and clarify a subject otherwise lost in darkness. He even attempted a vaguely oriental use of spatial perspective.

But the challenge proved too great for the time allowed him, and the book failed to sell, and was quickly remaindered. Critics too were far from kind. The conservative *Athenaeum* pronounced the stories alone "more grim than weird". The *Book Lover's Magazine* dismissed the book as "extraordinarily repulsive"; and by association Laurence's drawings suffered as well: "Dante did not traverse the *Inferno*

Housman's illustrations to Jonas Lie, Weird Tales from Northern Seas, *1893.*
a) *Frontispiece "The Gan-Fin"*
b) *"The Twelve Cormorants"*
c) *"The Wind Gnome"*
d) *"The Huldrefish"*

unscathed, and Mr Housman has not wholly escaped contamination from the abominable regions explored by Mr Bain." Only in later years, when critics could judge the drawings against future work, did they find elements of importance in these "quite boyish designs, in which we see none-the-less the strength coming".[33]

Despite the book's failures, it gave Laurence a taste of illustrating on a large scale, and he found the challenge more sympathetic to his skills than designing book bindings and title pages for Lane. He decided if he chose a subject to illustrate without the constraints of publisher deadlines and a set format, he might have a greater chance of success. Within a month of the publication of Weird Tales, he wrote John Lane of his new idea, proposing a suitably Blakeian subject for a book. "Do you think 'Illustrations to the Book of Jonah' would take on? a small book done some-what in the [William] Morris style with very big heavy lettering for the page and about 15 illustrations, also 'big' and heavy, done by me." Knowing the text was short, he proposed he might "spin it out" with large drawings to fill a book. "The proportion of page to be like the 'Canterbury Poets' series only a good bit larger – Thompson Poems only a little smaller. This is a mere suggestion: I know I should like doing it; but I know nothing of the market." It was a humble suggestion – that in the end he would bow to Lane's superior judgement. Even if the idea was accepted he could not start work until the summer, "as I am full up". Unfortunately the book never materialized.[34]

As the projects and commissions grew, Laurence found he had to plan his work time carefully to complete his deadlines. Yet always at the back of his mind was the idea for a book of his own, proposed, drawn and submitted to a publisher in his own time. As early as the spring of 1893, while still working for Lane, he devised a book idea which was to become a labour of love and prove a turning point in his bid for public acceptance of his illustrations. He had long admired the poetry of Christina Rossetti; "the sort of nonsense that is worth writing", according to Alfred. One

Rossetti's two illustrations to Goblin Market, *1862.*

of her most enchanting poems, *Goblin Market*, had been illustrated with just two drawings by her brother, Dante Gabriel, some thirty years earlier, and Laurence admired these, but felt a larger, fully illustrated version was now needed. He wrote to propose the project to Miss Rossetti's publisher, George Macmillan, hoping to gain permission to use the poem. Macmillan was a stranger to him at the time, and in his second, more detailed letter, he attempted to introduce himself as a professional illustrator with serious intentions. He had carefully studied the poem and believed a "medieval" approach to the drawings would be most suitable (surely a safe bet knowing his predecessor's passion for the period). To enhance his proposal he sent a series of rough sketches with his 20 March letter, explaining, "The sketches I have mounted, to indicate the size of the page I would like to suggest, and also the arrangement, in certain cases, of illustrations facing each other and forming two halves as it were of one picture — a revival of a medieval usage which I think might be made effective and pleasant." The key to the project he knew would be the goblins. His solution to the problem of how best to indicate their symbolic role in the story was to give them masks; a "pictorial allegory" borrowed from his theatrical past and love of Greek drama.

"I have imagined goblins wearing animal masks in order to hide the wickedness that their own faces would reveal; this will give me the opportunity of a dramatic climax when in the poem they are finally defeated by Lizzie. I propose then to show them throwing aside their masks as they make their escape. I hope Miss Rossetti will not think this idea is in any disagreement with the spirit of her poem."[35]

His enthusiasm for the project was tested during the month it took to receive the publisher's reply. On 18 April he learnt from Macmillan, "The matter has been under the author's consideration and as you know we could come to no decision until we knew her views. They are not on the whole unfavourable to the idea, but she cannot bring herself to sanction the 'masks' which you introduce in your treatment of the goblins. 'They might' Miss R. writes, 'illustrate some better poem, but mine they falsify. Would not a study of my goblins as they stand supply an adequate variety of versatility of expression, a roguishness easily transformable into atrocity?' She then refers to her brother's original frontispiece." Macmillan then proposed that Laurence might make a new specimen goblin drawing without its mask, which could be sent to Miss Rossetti for approval. This he did, and on 16 May he received the long awaited news that she agreed to the book: "I am fully satisfied...I am obliged to Mr Housman for his compliance with my wish, and assure him that my goblin will keep peace with all his."[36]

Once he obtained final permission, the difficulty again was to find enough time to complete the drawings. It was his most ambitious project to date, eventually totalled thirty-three text drawings, four full page, four double page illustrations as well as a cover, half-title and title page designs. They marked a change in Laurence's style and suggested a greater confidence in figure drawing, with their firm outlines, even shading and inventive characterizations all drawn for the wood engraver. He paid homage to Rossetti's heavy medieval woodcut style, and retained his mentor's cuddly, childish vision of the goblins as lovable creatures of the woods. Laurence gave them cat-like and bird features, borrowed from rats, moles and weasels for the furry impression of harmlessness which so effectively contrasted with the sinister motives of the goblins, their wide, blank eyes intent on luring the unsuspecting sisters in the story. He dressed them in voluminous drapery and wide brimmed hats to add to the sense of mystery. The squat, hunched goblins became a challenge to his skills of shading for the wood engraver as well. Later one critic in *The Studio* objected to this trick of "uniform dark outlining that rendered it difficult to see the figures in their right planes, so that they looked rather cramped within their few inches of space". But the drawings remain some of his richest, most inventive creations.

The story of *Goblin Market* appealed yet again to his "freakish imagination". It was a tale of sisterly devotion in the face of forbidden evils; those symbolic passions offered by the soul-stealing goblin creatures of the wood. Moreover, the theme of an older sister's devotion and love of her younger sister clearly echoed Laurence's own domestic bliss, just as the poem ended in a sisterly pledge of loyalty:

"For there is no friend like a sister
In calm or stormy weather;
To cheer one on the tedious way
To fetch one if one goes astray
To lift one if one totters down,
To strengthen whilst one stands."

And Laurence seemed to suggest this affinity in his sympathetic drawings of the two sisters, as one critic shrewdly pointed out: "The goblins, pale-eyed, mole and rat and weasel-faced; the sisters, whose simple life they surround with hideous fantasy, are realised in harmony with the unique effect of the poem — an effect of simplicity, of naive imagination, of power, of things stranger than are told in the cry of the goblin merchants, as at evening time they invade quiet places to traffic with their evil fruits for the souls of maidens."[37]

The book appeared in December 1893, and received the most critical attention of all the designs Laurence published that year. The green cloth binding he devised, with its medieval strap-work and gilt stamped plant-form pattern overall, had been exhibited at the Arts and Crafts Exhibition

Housman's binding design for Goblin Market, *1893.*

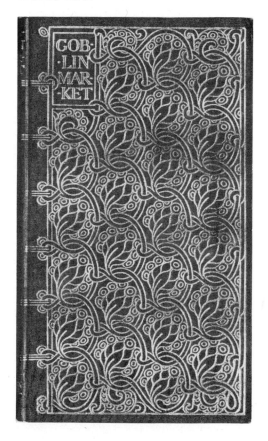

in October, and attracted a large number of admirers when *The Studio* reproduced it in their review of the exhibition. The published drawings produced substantial reviews (see critical chapter below), and brought Laurence's skills to the attention of some of the period's most influential artists. Sir Frederic Leighton, pillar of the art world and President of the Royal Academy, became a patron. He was always in search of such impressive new talent, and had commissioned drawings from Ricketts and Beardsley at £5 each. After studying *Goblin Market*, he sent Laurence a similar offer of praise and admiration, and asked for one of the original drawings to add to his collection. Eventually he bought the title page design because, as Laurence later proudly explained, "what struck him most in my work was the combination of figures with decoration". But the most critical opinion, that of the book's author, proved the one real disappointment. She never explained her reactions to Laurence, but he learnt from a secondary source that she was far from pleased: "I had hoped to get word that my drawings had pleased her; but the only comment that reached me was her answer to a congratulating friend who liked them. She shook her head, saying, 'I don't think my Goblins were quite so ugly'."[38]

John Lane continued to dominate Laurence's career, and by early 1894, after spending the Christmas holidays going through Clemence's stories, Laurence decided to share his influential patron with her. He wrote Lane about a cycle of four stories Clemence had written under the title "Strange Women", and hoped Lane would agree to publish them. "I am almost tired of telling people how much better I think her work than my own, and beyond that, being her brother, I had better be silent." He admitted they were experimental, one involved "modern problems in an old dress", and had been rejected by "one or two publishers who have seen it seem scandalized at her solution of it. I don't think you will be, and

Housman's Goblin Market *illustrations.*

Title page design for Katharine Tynan Hinkson, Cuckoo Songs, *1894.*

therefore [I] offer it [to] you". Lane's response was courteous when he asked to see more stories. But he did not publish them, and it was only some two years later that he agreed to publish Laurence's illustrated edition of Clemence's *The Were-Wolf.*[39]

He continued to commission book designs from Laurence, however. The cover design and title page to Katharine Tynan Hinkson's *Cuckoo Songs* appeared in February 1894. One of Laurence's boldest title pages, he used a heavy outline in his new Goblin Market style for the Pre-Raphaelite maiden seated beneath an open bottle-glass casement window, playing a lute. The flow of her robe matched the twist of the tree-like vine device he devised to unify the upper block of text; while the book title was engraved on a stone wall, with the author and publisher names set in a scroll-like rectangle in the lower left hand corner.

Lane was obviously pleased with the result and he paid Laurence his fee within a week of receiving his account.

But Lane was not always so easily pleased. Laurence was increasingly fond of symbols which he drew into the frontispieces he sent Lane for approval. They were his attempt at combining his literary inclinations after reading a book's text, with his artistic instincts for obscure symbols, and the result was often difficult to understand. Too often he viewed the concept of temptation and evil as a nude figure, often in suggestive poses, and this upset the more restrained sensibilities of John Lane (who was after all the son of a Devonshire yeoman farmer) with rather conservative tastes when it came to upsetting his buying public. Laurence experienced his first bout of Lane's censorship when his original frontispiece design for Thompson's *Poems* was rejected by Lane. He had called the drawing "The Reflected Faun", which depicted a number of male nudes posed alongside a stream. Lane objected and Laurence provided the second drawing, of just two male figures, one nude, the other heavily draped which was published. But Laurence refused to forget the offending drawing and when Aubrey Beardsley approached him for a drawing for *The Yellow Book*, Lane's newest venture with Beardsley appointed as art editor, Laurence sent "The Reflected Faun". Beardsley had in fact admired his Goblin Market drawings, and Laurence hoped this more obviously sensual subject would be accepted, which it was. It appeared in that first scandalous issue of *The Yellow Book*, in April 1894, alongside drawings by Beardsley, Pennell, Rothenstein, Anning Bell, and for respectability, a frontispiece by Leighton.

The reception of *The Yellow Book* and its rebellious young art editor's disregard for his employer's policies — in the end Lane was forced to search each proposed drawing with a magnifying glass and consult a jury of like-minded friends to advise him before publication — encouraged Laurence's own rebellious attitude toward John Lane. When his drawing appeared in the *Yellow Book* he was immediately associated with this new sensational journal: "It was newness *in excelsis*: novelty naked and unashamed. People were puzzled and shocked and delighted, and yellow became the colour of the hour, the symbol of the time-spirit. It was associated with all that was *bizarre* and queer in art life, with all that was outrageously modern."[40] Following publication of the 'Reflected Faun', Laurence wrote to Lane in an unrepentent tone, asking for the return of the drawing, which he thought he could now sell. "An art-patron has turned up who has an indiscriminate wish to possess 'something' of mine, and this may do for him." He added a jocular note about the *Yellow Book:* "By the way are you not going to 'compliment' me with a copy of 'The Yellow Book'. I see it is out: rumour says running into editions. One or two printers and publishers have abused it in my hearing, which is a wholesome sign."[41]

The incident marked the beginning of a strain in his relations with Lane, which he discovered while working on his next commission. When asked to provide the usual cover, frontispiece and title page designs to a new Francis Thompson volume, *Sister Songs*, he began the frontispiece drawing first, as was his habit. Perhaps he was buoyed by the reception of the *Yellow Book*, or perhaps he felt Lane could not now object to a similar drawing since he had in essence published the early one and finally given it his approval. Whatever his motive, Laurence again upset Lane with another scandalous nude drawing. He called it "Barren Life", and it depicted a male nude encircled in rose thorns, surrounded by symbolic nude figures of evil and a Pan-like earth god. He had thought a great deal about this composition and tried to symbolize Thompson's religious poems and bring to them his own intense religious obsession, which he based on the image of Christ's crucifixion. Lane failed to see the value, apart from obvious scandal, in the drawing; but this time instead of outright rejection, he asked for Laurence's detailed explanation of the symbols. Fortunately this survives to indicate the sincerity of Laurence's motives, and the continued thoroughness with which

*Housman's censored drawing "Barren Life",
in* The Yellow Book, *1896.*

he attacked each new Lane commission:

"The full figure in my drawing represents a human soul bound among thorns and roses to the doorway of life. At his touch the roses of pleasure crumble and fall; pleasure has become suffering; this I have ventured to suggest under the form of the crucifixion, as I wished to put in contrast the crucified sinner and the crucified Sinless One.

"To the left is a figure that represents man's lower nature, once the tempter, and now the scoffer at the soul's sufferings. He holds the wine up and the thyrsus. In the latter my idea has been to give a parallel to the sponge set upon a reed in which the vinegar was offered to Christ.

"To the right sits Nature or Flora, a neutral figure, capable of good or evil, holding Pan's pipes among a lap full of flowers. But behind her stands St Eustace's Stag, representing Nature's spiritual side and the revelation, through Nature, of Christ. This touch, so strong in 'The

Hound of Heaven' [Thompson's poem], seem to me to be everywhere in Thompson's writing. The pair of doves flying toward the soul's heart as messengers of comfort hardly require any explanation in connection with the present volume."

He openly admitted the impossibility of making all his symbols apparent to the reader in just one full-page illustration; but he insisted this must be his goal, to summarize the religious theme in Thompson's poems. "My difficulty, I found, was to illustrate the whole book. If I illustrated one section, I ignored the other: and indeed, from the merely incidental point of view the poems seem to me to be only the means for giving expression to a very inward and spiritual line of thought, difficult to state, even in allegory and symbolism, but impressive and extremely personal. I was the less unwilling to attempt my somewhat personal reading as Thompson has himself been so much more personal in his expression throughout the poems." His concluding defence was the one unfortunate remark Lane finally used to reject the drawing: "There are one or two smaller touches, such as the leafless and barren thorns girding the loins into which I need not perhaps enter." And in the end he remained convinced, "I think I have given you a sufficiently general view of the meaning of the whole".[42]

The full reason Lane rejected the drawing remains a mystery. According to Lane's biographer and early associate, "a lamentable fate overtook this beautiful picture. For some inexplicable reason Lane got it into his head, or had it put there, that the drawing was indecent and another picture to take its place was hurriedly designed by the justly annoyed and bewildered artist." But in the end Laurence had the last word yet again, and "Barren Life" was published by Beardsley in the *Yellow Book*, in the summer of 1896.

Tailpiece from Goblin Market, *1893*.

The Voice of the Fairies

hen the pressure of publisher deadlines, financial struggles and thwarted ambitions seemed almost too much to bear, Laurence characteristically turned to his writing for escape. He found a strange comfort in fantasy, after having learnt to depend upon fairy tales as a young boy disillusioned with the real world. It allowed him to retain a childish nature, and became his most valued asset while composing those fairy tales and myths which eventually made his reputation as a writer.

Many of these early stories had been inspired by Clemence's peculiar taste for the bizarre, the passionate and the religious. Laurence in fact dedicated several of his more poetic tales to her, clearly indebted to her for inspiration. She had an "inborn appetite, which she never lost, for heroes and heroines in suffering for the sins of others", he later recalled. Even Alfred admired her self-sacrificing approach to life, once describing her as "Clemence becomes a fancied knight/In visionary armour dight..." A poet as well as a prose writer, she replaced Alfred as Laurence's mentor, up to a point: "About my poetry she told me afterwards that she had been very much afraid I should never get away from my Byron stage; but she did not damp my ardour with her doubts," Laurence insisted.[1] Mostly she shared his passionate desire for characterization. Together they wanted to know how their creations felt, what made them do the things they did, whether they possessed an inner life of the emotions, which unfortunately had to be masked by social conventions. It is perhaps not surprising that Clemence found her brother Alfred a mystery. His obsessive privacy in London was a puzzle which she failed to solve. Only when she read his *A Shropshire Lad,* in a mixture of sorrow and relief did she exclaim, "Alfred has a heart". Later, after Alfred's death, Laurence decided to destroy his brother's deeply personal poetry notebooks and papers, and did it "thinking of Clem". Only afterwards he thought "it may have been a mistake".

Such was the hold his sympathetic sister had over them. It explains why Laurence would always be devoted to his beloved "Clem". He admired her skills as a fantasy writer, and after publication of "The Were-Wolf" in *Atalanta,* he proposed an illustrated book edition to John Lane. It was one of their most successful collaborations, Laurence's six full page drawings replacing the previous magazine illustrations by Everard Hopkins. His critics declared them "among the treasures of those who collect his 'early period' ". He devised a simple cover design (the title gilt-stamped on pink cloth), a title-page printed in orange, and various initial letters to again fit the Lane formula for unity in book design. They enhanced the grisly tale of the she-wolf White Fell which, because Clemence had set it in some remote northern land, resembled the Norse legends then so popular with William

a) "White Fell's Escape"

b) "The Race"

c) "The Finish"

d) "Sweyn's Finding"

Morris and his followers. Clemence used the story of devoted twin brothers – one murdered by the she-wolf and discovered by his horror-struck other brother – to create passages of powerful religious symbols: Sweyn discovers his brother Christian lying in a pool of his own blood on the snow, "the figure of one crucified, the blood-stained hands also conforming". The image unified the story: in a neat twist of evangelical plotting Sweyn "knew surely that to him Christian had been as Christ, and had suffered and died to save him from his sins".[2]

Unlike Laurence, Clemence was a slow writer and generally worked at night, sometimes fortified by a glass of scotch and the silence of London, asleep outside her window. As a result she published just three books and a few suffragette articles. *The Were-Wolf* was followed by the equally haunting tale, *The Unknown Sea*, 1898, a story of self-sacrifice and bitterness, with echoes of her own private yearnings to escape the stifling atmosphere of Perry Hall. She wrote it in a vivid, if not lurid style, which shocked her more inhibited critics, with phrases like "the incurable wounds of a proud spirit, gaped and bled hot and fresh". It was the story of a souless, naked siren adrift on an island, who was visited by a young innocent fisherman. He undergoes terrible "physical and moral" ordeals, which allowed for some striking contrasts with the mysterious natural forces of the sea. In the end, the pagan villagers, with their religious rites, become responsible for the spiritual birth of the siren, and the martyrdom of the young fisherman. It made strange if eccentric reading; a religious tract with the colourful eccentricity of an adventure story, where reality mixed with the supernatural.

Following another prolonged writing session, which stretched over fourteen years, she published a medieval romance, *The Life of Sir Aglovale de Galis*, in 1905. It was in fact a psychological reconstruction of the Morte d'Arthur legend,

Housman's illustrations to
The Were-Wolf, *1896:*

which shocked readers steeped in Victorian concepts of Arthurian chivalry and honour by arguing the real reason for the breakup of Arthur's court was his incest and Lancelot's adultery. Laurence admired her courage and pronounced it "something better than I have ever done". But such an unpopular view shocked critics and a public still under the spell of Tennyson's idealized vision of Arthur. The story was largely ignored and only when it was republished in 1953 were critics given a second chance "to appraise its excellence", according to the DNB. She had greater success in America, where her allegorical story "The Drawn Arrow" appeared in an anthology, *31 Stories by 31 Authors*, 1923, and much later her werewolf story was reprinted in 1974 (in which the foreward called Clemence "he"). She eventually gave up her writing for more urgent concerns, like her suffragette activities and tending the household during the difficult wartime years. But she continued to advise Laurence on his own writing until her death.

The medievalism he so much admired in his sister's stories was adopted for his own purposes as well. He studied the woodcuts of Dürer, and woodcut borders of fine printed books recently adapted by William Morris and Charles Ricketts to give their printing a romantic appeal. They appealed to his own romantic view of life at the time: "Romantic in temperament, and religiously sentimental in my upbringing, I began by preferring things medieval to things modern," he recalled. "My poems, fairy tales, and legends were nearly all idealistic and fanciful — away from reality."[3] He devised stories with maidens in distress or chivalric heroes of unsuspecting humbleness, and set his tales in enchanted gardens or beneath the walls of some imaginary medieval city. He intended these "fairy tales and dreamy poems of another world" for children, and critics compared the best of them to Hans Andersen or even Oscar Wilde. But his use of symbols, poetic imagery and occasional lapses into literary vocabulary indicated he sought a more educated adult audience as well. The tales were eventually collected together and illustrated in four volumes. His critics admired them for their imaginative powers and the strange, inventive illustrations; "a long line of queerly original fairy tales, of which the sometimes queerer illustrations [were] by himself", according to *The Times*.

He soon was associated with the world of fairy literature, and brought to his elfin creatures a refreshing sense of oneness, as if he had some secret power bestowed upon him. Once one of his admirers asked how he managed to draw and write about fairies so accurately, and he merely shrugged and said, "I always seem to have had it". The voice of the fairies was a great comfort; and it gave his critics as well as admirers a chance to label him as a unique fantasy writer: "Mr Housman is strangely at home in fairyland. There is, in fact, something distinctly uncanny about this obvious and serious familiarity with a place that is not a place 'within the meaning of the Act' ".⁴ It was a subject which inspired one of his most delightful stories, "A Capful of Moonshine", first published in *The Dome*, 1898. In this attempt to recapture the spirit of the traditional fairy-tale, he begins with a faggot-maker, who asks of an old man, "How is it that one gets to see a fairy?" To which the old man answers, "There are some to whom it comes by nature; but for others three things are needed – a handful of courage, a mouthful of silence, and a capful of moonshine."

Beneath the poetic language and atmospheric drawings lay Laurence's private conviction that a fairy-tale could teach a concept of morality he found lacking in organized religion. "The true end and object of a fairy-tale is the expression of the joy of living. There begins and ends the morality of the fairy-tale: its value consists in its optimism. So for the true and unpolluted air of fairyland we have to go back to the old and artless tales of a day purer and simpler than our own; purer because so wholly unconcerned with any questions of morals, simpler because so wholly unconcious of its simplicity."⁵ As one admirer pointed out perceptively, he was intentionally "luring the world to Old Religion by way of a walk through Fairyland".⁶

Between 1894 and 1904, Laurence produced a string of fairy-tales which were collected into four illustrated volumes: *A Farm in Fairyland*, 1894; *The House of Joy*, 1895; *The Field of Clover*, 1898; and *The Blue Moon*, 1904. Later other volumes were compiled from these and some remain in print today (see appendix for full list). As a whole, they represent the work of an imaginative writer with an eye and an ear for detail; the telling phrase, the delicate expression, with which he enchanted his young readers. His prose is musical and essentially simple, but nevertheless filled with action to stimulate a child's roving mind. The fate of a character can change within the twist of a phrase, the plot sent racing down an altogether new path. For those more interested in the sound of words and variety of colourful images, as was the popular preoccupation of the day, he was a master, whom Oscar Wilde praised. His atmospheric descriptions in "The Green Gaffer" Wilde found of "spellbinding beauty", and urged Laurence to follow this natural talent for poetry. Even today historians of children's literature include Housman's fairy-tales in anthologies because of his ability to delight the senses. Colours and textures preoccupied him: the magical white doe in "The Blue Moon" story drinks from a forest pool filled with fallen autumnal leaves which turn the water "the colour of blood"; or the blue moon itself is "hung like a burning grape against the sky. Like the heart of a sapphire laid open, the air flushed and purpled to a deeper shade." His images work on the reader to create a new world of enchantment out of familiar objects. In a forest where trees turn blue in the moonlight, like peacock feathers, they "seemed carved out of blue stone...Jewel within jewel they burned through every shade from beryl to onyx. The white blossoms of a cherry-tree had become changed into turquoise, the tossing spray

---

A passion for medievalism and Dürer's woodcuts inspired Housman's "The Invisible Princess", an illustration to "Blind Love", in The Pageant, *1897.*

Elements of Housman's style:

a) Grotesque detail and concentrated lighting were borrowed from Arthur Boyd Houghton and the Sixties School, for "Tug of War", in Weird Tales, *1893.*

b) The open window device from the Dutch school used for "Rocking Horse Land", in A Farm in Fairyland, *1894.*

---

of a fountain as it drifted and swung was like a column of blue fire."

The characters in his stories search for beauty and happiness rather than the more mundane struggles for wealth or power. In "The Rooted Lover", for example, a humble ploughboy pines for the love of a beautiful princess he has never met but only admires from a hole in the garden hedge. He turns himself into a scarlet poppy which attracts her attention and eventually wins her love. Or there is the tale of a plain Japanese woman, who marries a wind spirit and has its child. Each day he visits her from the clouds, and when she is condemned to death, in the end he rescues her from the executioner and she floats up to join her family. Each volume contained a number of curious creatures as well: from a greedy gold-obsessed rat-catcher who sells his beauti-

ful daughter to a gold-miner gnome, to twelve bald princesses cursed by the nocturnal thief who steals their hair for a tapestry.

The illustrations he devised to accompany each story were usually full-page engravings placed as frontispieces to intro-

---

c) Japanese prints inspired the bold spatial composition in "The Parlous Tree", in A Farm in Fairyland, *1894.*

d) An ideal, formal Italianate garden and medieval maiden for "The Moon-Flower", in The House of Joy, *1895.*

e) Classical sculpture inspired the reclining figure in "Syringa", from The House of Joy, *1895.*

f) A claustrophobic interior borrowed from Rossetti, the swirling drapery from Arthur Hughes for "The Crown's Warranty", in The Field of Clover, *1898.*

c)

d)

e)

f)

duce each tale. They were not intended to present each character or incident in the stories, but rather attempts to suggest the tone of the story: the quiet sadness of the plain Japanese woman always alone with her thoughts; the magical world of the princess's garden seen over the top of the hedge by the love-sick ploughboy. They are pastiches culled from numerous sources: the classical severity of Renaissance architecture, the pure innocence of Botticelli's maidens, the stark silhouettes and absence of spatial definition from Greek vases, the claustrophobia and minute detail of Dutch interiors, and regimented formality of Italian gardens. His clipped hedges, rose standards and marble fountains are liberally sprinkled across backgrounds which suggest a basic sense of perspective, or in some cases the Japanese reversal of space. He incorporated figures with hard firm lines borrowed from Dürer, as well as the frizzy-haired Pre-Raphaelite maidens and classical aesthetic heroes of his mentors Rossetti or Sandys. They are drawn in the dense pen work of Hughes, Walker and Houghton; the landscapes and rural settings done in homage to Pinwell and Walker. There is even a hint of the suggestive exoticism of Beardsley and Moreau in his elongated figures and tapestries encrusted in floral patterns.

He was most influenced in these fairy illustrations by an earlier master of the genre, Arthur Hughes. "It was my great good fortune to be brought up from my earliest years on the illustrations," he proudly recalled. Later he wrote about them in *The Bibliophile,* to encourage a revival of interest in this master. He most admired "their almost perfect adjustment of means to end, and the singular element of beauty which underlies their simple craftsmanship". By studying Hughes, the reader gained a new dimension to the story, for his drawings were not realistic imitations of conventional objects; they used an "arbitrary disposal of light and shade" and avoided form and texture to concentrate upon the impression of an ethereal, non-material world. This was essential to fairy illustration; it helped "assist the mind to ascertain independence of material things, and thus, for the reader of the books which they illustrate, they produce what they are meant to produce — a fairy world. A fairy world which stands the test of years." In addition, Hughes chose a child's-eye view of the world to challenge his young readers, exaggerating figures and extending their shadows, selecting his details carefully. "The flat, forbidding obscurity of night, pallor of moonlight, the radiant centrality of daylight and fire" were the tricks Laurence decided Hughes had devised to make him a master fairy illustrator: "the flash of a magic jewel, the motion of light and wind amid flowing hair, to all that may arrest the attention of imaginative childhood and awaken its sense of romance".[7]

Hughes had also taught him "the power of identifying himself with his subject"; a valuable lesson which Laurence combined with his own rather unorthodox drawing technique. He turned his back on the conventional lessons of his art school, where the study from diagrams and models resulted in perfect, though uninspired copies. He sought to reverse the process, using the search for expression and an individual style as his goals. He was always fond of the epigram, "Nature is not a fit subject for art, but may be a very useful medium". He began each drawing with an impressionistic sketch from memory, then, if necessary, he compared it with a life model, a flower, or published drawing, painting or woodcut. This allowed him the essential freedom of expression which, although it preserved "certain lapses of truth", he compensated for such inaccuracy with a freshness and individualism which became hallmarks of his decorative style. He concentrated upon detail; those intricate surfaces which allowed him to gloss over obvious anatomical errors; taking his greatest inspiration from the Pre-Raphaelites and Sixties School illustrators. Their wood engraved drawings were masterpieces of detail, where it was "difficult to find even a square inch of blank space left to represent ground or sky; they worked with jewel-like effect, regarding the wood they drew on as a sort of precious metal whose surface was too much value to be thrown away". Clemence's experience as a wood engraver of such detailed work must have provided him with valuable assistance in early works; later he produced drawings almost exclusively for her graver. But in the end he remained convinced of the value of those first "rapid, nervous sketches and studies" which gave little hint of the finished drawing, but guided his imagination to eliminate the unnecessary, the accademic, and the over-fussy.

And yet Laurence was secretive about technique, especially how he built up his drawings from these early sketches. He never discussed his methods, perhaps preferring to leave unexplained that essential element of chance and the unexpected so necessary for their creation. The only brief hint we have was given to his admirer Gleeson White during his preparations for an article about Housman's illustrations. White was shown the original ink drawings for several fairy tales used in *A Farm in Fairyland* and *The House of Joy*, and was surprised to discover how much more considered their densely packed surfaces were. "Drawn very slightly larger than they appear in the reproduction" (since they were process engraved), White concluded "it seems barely possible that the complex and exquisitely minute detail could be achieved by ordinary eyesight. Yet as a matter of fact, they were." He asked Laurence to explain "how the delicate minuteness of these could be set down without a magnifying glass", and he received a characteristic, vague answer: "I think I have eyes at the tips of my fingers, I seem to feel the line even if I can hardly see it." And in the end, it was the extreme delicacy of such detail, however it was produced, which enhanced the stories they illustrated.[8]

His first important fairy illustration commission was to an edition of Jane Barlow's *The End of Elfin-Town,* 1894. Alongside his *Goblin Market* drawings, the eight full-page, six large text drawings, title-page, cover and dustwrapper designs rank among his best known work. The commission came from Macmillans, obviously pleased with his *Goblin Market* work. He planned a number of intricate

woodland and floral settings for this tale of elfin frolics, drawn in his new confident outline style. He borrowed from Beardsley for the winged title-page figures, as well as Ricketts for his dense ink-work detail. He took great care drawing the pointed-eared elfin creatures, which he placed in accurate settings to allow for the sense of contrast between the real and the imaginary world. His elves dance in pools of light, or fly with dragon-fly like wings for that sense of light, ethereal unworldliness essential to the verse story. He sought that quality in flowers and foliage, and in one instance found it in the downy tufts of dandelion seed heads, which he planned to draw in a grouping around the elves, until he realised the problem of light falling upon the globes needed further study. He knew he would have to abandon his schedule and find a botanical book in the art library at South Kensington, and just as he was about to leave an unexpected woman visitor knocked at his door. She wore a hat trimmed in

Title design to Jane Barlow's The End of Elfin-Town, *1894.*

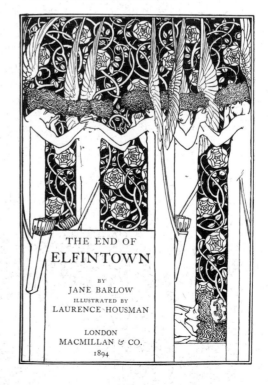

THE END OF
ELFINTOWN

BY
JANE BARLOW
ILLUSTRATED BY
LAURENCE HOUSMAN

LONDON
MACMILLAN & CO.
1894

A perfect Pre-Raphaelite maiden, "The Rat-Catcher's Daughter", sacrificed to the ugly gold-hoarding gnome, from The Blue Moon, *1904. A good example of*

Housman's delicate penwork. Original pen and ink drawing on brown paper, 6 x 3⅝" Tate Gallery.

The End of Elfin-Town, *1894:*
a) "The Building"

b) "The Council"

c) "The Flitting"

d) Text drawing

II.—THE COUNCIL

"The Council", from
The End of Elfin-Town, *1894.*

'what o'clocks', or dandelion seed tufts, and Laurence stared at it in disbelief. "God has sent you!" he gasped and before he could explain he sat her in a chair by the window and insisted she model it for him. The result was "The Council", a full-page drawing of elves set among the delicate stems and tufts of a dandelion wood. It was praised for its "strangeness in beauty"; one critic called it an example of masterly illustration which "should be studied" by those less imaginative or daring.[9]

Much of the strength of his fairy illustrations came from the overt symbolism used to emphasize a mood or a subject. He gave a large amount of space to these drawings – usually full-page opposite the text – to allow his readers the full opportunity of study; or he repeated the most symbolic

Frontispiece and title designs for
A Farm in Fairyland, *1894.*

ones as a frontispiece, surrounded by an elaborate interlace or strapwork borders which stretched double-page to incorporate the title-page as well. This formula first appeared in *A Farm in Fairyland*, 1894, a compilation of twelve fairy-tales with their own full-page illustrations, published by Kegan Paul. Here the frontispiece "The Rooted Lover" doubles as an illustration to one of the most enchanting of the stories drawn with an intriguing use of symbolism. The young lover views his forbidden princess through a high hedge which splits the composition diagonally to reveal two worlds. Other such imaginative devices were used on the remainder of the twelve illustrations to the stories, each of which were dedicated to a child. They are a delightful collection of characters, from the mystic glamour of Japonel, the greedy woodcutter's daughter, to the stories of a

"The Horse with the Hump", from
A Farm in Fairyland, *1894.*

horse with an unfortunate hump, a green bird, and a grotesque tale of the man who killed a cuckoo. And while these characters are often only suggested or overlooked altogether, a number of familiar symbols to describe their moods recur in the drawings: the clipped hedge surrounding the idyllic garden of the frontispiece, in which maidens in diaphanous gowns stroll in the shadow of a medieval city; or in later works a pastoral landscape was a favourite device, borrowed from Renaissance paintings. His gardens of hedge roses echo the Victorian symbol of perfect domestic beauty; the walls and high hedges with occasional gaps or doorways were well-established symbols of the outside world, where love, temptation and freedom await. Laurence borrowed such symbols from his beloved Pre-Raphaelites, most notably Rossetti, whom he admired for drawings

"Japonel", from
A Farm in Fairyland, *1894.*

Frontispiece and title designs for
The House of Joy, *1895.*

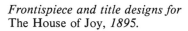

that could recreate "the drift of an entire poem within the space of a single picture". Another favourite Rossetti device was spatial contrast: a heavily draped woman with long hair crouches in a dark, low-ceilinged room, with only an open window to relieve the claustrophobia. Such stifling confinement enhanced a story's sense of foreboding and charged the reader with a sense of expectancy, just as Laurence had earlier done in the crowded drawings to *Goblin Market*.

The following year a second collection of fairy-tales, *The House of Joy,* was again published by Kegan Paul. Here eight stories had their own full-page illustrations wood engraved by Clemence. The title-page adopted the familiar winged Mercury-cum-ploughman figure of the first volume, but here he was standing before one of those familiar Rossetti maidens imprisoned behind a heavy carved doorway, her arms

appealing to him from her tiny open window. This and the opposite frontispiece – a medieval forest scene, homage to Burne-Jones – were surrounded by a delicate Celtic strapwork border which was praised by Gleeson White for its "sure mastery of line". The overall sense of delicacy challenged the established heavy medievalism of William Morris; and yet the fine ink line of the border was still compatible with the heavier surfaces of the illustrations, themselves "sheer marvels of craft, so delicate in their line and crowded with intricate pattern, that the elaborate borders seem simple by comparison".

The illustrations are some of Laurence's most considered and intricate. The foliage backgrounds of varying textures also show the expertise of Clemence's engraving technique. She inspired the delightful story, "The Luck of the Roses", about a garden of red roses turned white by the death of a fairy, which Laurence dedicated to her. The accompanying drawing, of a couple bathed in lantern light as they peer at the fairy spirit, is a masterwork of light and dark, a homage to Hughes as well as Dürer and Rembrandt. Here too is the equally evocative "Happy Returns", a story of old age and youthfulness when a fisherman discovers a magic fish. Laurence drew the grostesque atmosphere of the tale in a silhouette fisherman, his back turned to the viewer so that he becomes a mere rigid figure of terror, being rowed by the swirling fish-spirit into a pool of forbidding darkness. On the whole, this second fairy-tale collection strengthened Laurence's place in the world of illustration and story-writing. Although it received a mixed critical reception (see critic chapter below), his technical abilities were clearly recognised. Walter Crane chose to reproduce the frontispiece in his influential survey, *Of The Decorative Illustration of Books*, 1896. And yet again Leighton wrote to express his admiration, and pur-

"The Luck of the Roses (to Clemence)", from The House of Joy, *1895.*

chased the frontispiece drawing. Later two proof engravings were selected for exhibition at the Loan Exhibition of Modern Illustration at the Victoria and Albert Museum in 1900.

Three years later, a third story collection appeared as *The Field of Clover,* 1898. Again published by Kegan Paul and engraved by Clemence, it marked a public tribute by Laurence to his engraver sister, and was dedicated "To My Dear Wood-Engraver". Here too the frontispiece and title-page were surrounded by another intricate border, even more ornate and heavier than previous designs. The ten full-page illustrations and initial letters were also linked to this overall sense of weight and rich detail. It was a collection of just five stories, of which "The Bound Princess" was divided into various parts. Tales had evocative titles like "The Fire Eaters", which Laurence drew as a crowd of Chinese

"Happy Returns", from
The House of Joy, *1895.*

Frontispiece and title designs for
The Field of Clover, *1898.*

midgets who tumble into a cottage to gulp at the tongues of fire which eventually consume the building; or "The Galloping Plough", with the dullard Noodle astride his magic plough as he races away from his nasty employer. In "The Crown's Warranty", a Rossetti maiden bends over a small desk in a low room, lit only by the bottle-glass window and a flame from a candle in a bracket on the desk. Each illustration showed an even greater confidence in assimilating and turning his influences into his own distinctive style.

The fourth collection, *The Blue Moon*, appeared some time later, in 1904, published this time by John Murray. Here again Clemence engraved the ten drawings (including frontispiece and title-page) and initial letters to ten stories of even greater poetic power. The title story, "The Blue Moon", used colour imagery in a series of superb descriptions, as did "The White Doe". He adopted oriental themes for "The Way of the Wind" and "A Chinese

"The Bound Princess – The Fire Eaters",
from The Field of Clover, *1898.*

"The Bound Princess – The Galloping Plough", from The Field of Clover, *1898.*

"The Bound Princess – The Thirsty Well", from The Field of Clover, *1898.*

Fairy Tale". All the drawings were superbly engraved with a lighter touch, their dark passages relying upon stipple or grainy surfaces suggestive of lithography, to represent solid objects as seemingly dissimilar as stone walls, foliage, or candle light on drapery or flowing hair. This preserved that early sense of the ethereal he often lost in works with heavier black outlines; and they remain his most polished exercises in light and shadow. The collection also marked his firm place as a storyteller among his fellow writers, and brought several new and challenging commissions. A selection of tales from the *Arabian Nights* he "retold" with elaborate colour illustrations by Edmund Dulac in 1907, was an enormously successful giftbook and secured Dulac's reputation for future ventures in the field. Later still Laurence

"The Bound Princess – The Burning Rose", from The Field of Clover, *1898.*

"The Bound Princess – The Camphor Worm", from The Field of Clover, *1898.*

"The Wishing-Pot", from The Field of Clover, *1898.*

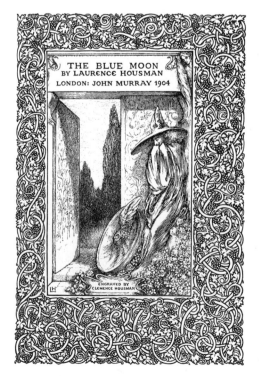

"A Capful of Moonshine", from
The Blue Moon, *1904.*

"A Chinese Fairy-tale", from
The Blue Moon, *1904.*

introduced another gift-book, the colour-plate edition of the *Rubáiyát of Omar Khayyám,* illustrated by Charles Robinson in 1928. His own stories were reissued in new anthologies as well, selected from the best of the previous four volumes (see appendix). He had clearly established a considerable reputation for his literary as well as artistic work. But with a character-istic air of discontent, he turned to further challenges – poetry and journalism. These he hoped would help him during those periods of financial worry which continued to plague his career.

Tailpiece from Goblin Market, *1893.*

Frontispiece and title designs to
The Blue Moon, *1904.*

*Original pen and ink drawing on brown
paper to "The White Doe", from* The Blue
Moon, *1904, 5½ x 3¼", Tate Gallery.*

Illustration from Goblin Market
Original colour wash by Gloria Cardew.

Illustration from Goblin Market
Original colour wash by Gloria Cardew.

Illustration from Goblin Market
Original colour wash by Gloria Cardew.

Illustration from Goblin Market
Original colour wash by Gloria Cardew.

Illustration from Goblin Market
Original colour wash by Gloria Cardew.

Illustration from Goblin Market
Original colour wash by Gloria Cardew.

Illustration from Goblin Market
Original colour wash by Gloria Cardew.

Illustration from Goblin Market
Original colour wash by Gloria Cardew.

A Poet and Critic

aurence had long been fascinated by poetry which challenged his descriptive abilities; it seemed the one medium which could combine visual preoccupations with his literary ambitions. Ever since those boyhood competitions set by Alfred and Clemence, he had written and studied poetry, he won school prizes for recitations, and later combined verses with his fairy stories. By the end of 1894, having completed his first volume of fairy-tales, he gathered together those poems he felt worthy of publication and sent them off to Alfred for comment.

Despite the fact that the brothers now rarely saw each other in London, it was at this time they felt a renewed affection for each other and their family. They shared a common grief when the death of their father was announced on 27 November 1894. This had come almost three weeks before Laurence's manuscript arrived at Alfred's, and served as a poignant reminder of the family tradition for verse writing. Their father, they recently discovered, had lived out his last years trying his own hand at verses, and even stole some of his son's poems, which he published under his own name in the local paper. Edward Housman's death was greeted with a mixture of sadness and relief by his family; "the removal of a burden and a distress" according to one sister, Kate. Surely the verses Laurence sent to Alfred, with their deeply personal pre-occupations with love and death, served

as fresh reminders of a shared loss; that of an eccentric and wholly lovable father.

When the manuscript arrived, Alfred was thinking over his own book of poems, which would eventually become *A Shropshire Lad*. His judgement was mixed now, but he was, as always, frank and sharp in his criticisms. Arranging Laurence's poems "in order of merit", he returned them with two long letters; "critical notes which I still cherish [which] were both kind and caustic", Laurence later recalled. He suggested which should be improved or eliminated. It was the first real sign of Alfred's interest in his brother's career; having taken up his post as Latin professor at University College, he continued to keep himself separate from his brother and sister in London. And yet, as he noticed Laurence's work received growing critical attention, he collected all his books in their various editions and sent copies of reviews to him. It was a mutual arrangement for which Laurence was always grateful: "I was conscious of having more regard for what Alfred would think and say of them than for what any other critic or the general public might think or say; for which reason even when our relations were not intimate, I generally sent to him for criticism all my books of verse before publication."[1]

The poems themselves were later described as "introspective glimpses of his own soul of a disturbing oddity" (DNB). They took as themes a favourite painting, like Millais's "Autumn Leaves", but more often were filled with painful sentimentality

Frontispiece and title designs for
Green Arras, *1896.*

---

or his own religious search, his doubts cloaked in obscure symbolism. Titles like "Loss and Gain" or "The Dead Mistress" echoed his growing preoccupation with the macabre or bizarre, and as one writer explained, "he has a distinct fondness, even a passion, for freaks of psychology; to his friends it often seemed that his own mind was essentially freakish".[2] Alfred found many verses too embarassing to publish; at best they upset his own obsession with personal privacy, or they were simply incomprehensible nonsense. Grateful as ever, Laurence accepted this judgement and eliminated several before publication.

He also planned to illustrate the book, and sent along proofs of his illustrations for Alfred's comments. Here again Alfred was harsh yet witty, and even sent his own sketches of subjects he felt should have been drawn (see critical chapter below for full remarks). The final selection of five full-page illustrations, forty-three initials,

endpapers, cover and title-page designs was published as *Green Arras*, by John Lane in 1896. The title suggested it was a tapestry of changing poetic patterns and Laurence drew a sinewy rose tree hung with a rose-patterned tapestry on the title page, with an oriental violinist playing to a bound (and symbolic) figure. Alfred did not like the fine gold interlace cover design on olive green cloth (a variant of *Goblin Market*), but Laurence thought it "very rich and elaborate", and it stayed. And in the end *Green Arras* was a labour of love, which combined the critical comments of his brother, the wood engravings of his sister (to whom the book was again dedicated), with his own ambitions as a poet.

Several other volumes of poems followed, so that in later years Laurence could dismiss this first as "not my serious work". Indeed, it sat unhappily in John Lane's list of poetry (his "nest of singing birds", as he called it). But it received a generous literary and critical reception, oversha-

---

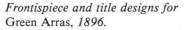

"Antaeus", from Green Arras, *1896.*

dowed only by the greater success of Alfred's *A Shropshire Lad,* (although this took some time in coming, and was not praised as openly when it first appeared). The *Athenaeum* critic praised Laurence's descriptive powers; "every poem or passage in which the author succeeds has the power of making us see a picture". The illustrations were less successful, especially his "Antaeus", which was attacked by the *Athenaeum* as an "insult to common as well as aesthetic sense". It was a daring attempt at innovation, the bold figure of Antaeus given an extraordinarily large head and posed in the foreground, his dwarf body entwined in vines suggestive of his earth-bound powers. ("Down in her darkness felt the Earth / The feet go by of one, whose birth / Claimed her his mother") Behind him rises a steep cliff, which soars off the page in a flagrant disregard of conventional perspective. But the Antaeus subject was a deeply personal one; later Laurence wrote an autobiographical novel,

"The House-Builders", from Green Arras, *1896.*

"The Corn-Keeper", from Green Arras, *1896.*

A Modern Antaeus, in which he figured as the young Antaeus, the country-born youth sent off to earn his living in the city, with disastrous consequences.

Here too appeared the strange and satisfying "The Corn Keeper", which one critic called "one of the most beautiful drawings...that the last decade of the nineteenth century produced from any hand".[3] It accompanied the haunting verse story of a corn blight,which lures a child's soul from its body ("I am sent to gather dreams,/ In among the white moonbeams") and fails to return the soul by daybreak; the child dying to universal lament. And it was his ability to marry poetic verse with evocative drawings – of fauns gazing into pools of shadow, birds soaring over a pale sky, or pairs of sorrowful lovers entwined in grief – which captured literary critics in Britain and, when published in Chicago, in America as well. Laurence was declared a poet as well as an illustrator: "We cannot yet place him among the great ones, but his genius and our justice alike in his relationships with fellow writers, began to grow as the result. The poet Edith Nesbit had written to Laurence her warm praises of his early verses published in the *Atalanta*, and they soon became good friends. But this lasted for only a short time. Laurence designed her bookplate and agreed to design her verse collection, *A Pomander of Verse*, published by John Lane in 1895. It was a delightful Lane commission, for which he devised a rose tapestry and elegant woman in flowing draperies on the title page. He recalled how Edith Nesbit became "one of my kindest and most generous friends in those early days"; until her demands for equal attention and praise of her own work proved too much for him. She "hungered for appreciation", he remembered with distaste; and how "liking her so much", he

"The Queen's Bees", from
Green Arras, *1896.*

forbid us to class him with the crowd of minor poets who sing nowadays in thin-voiced, many-throated, weariful chorus, and to whose metric ailments one longs to offer the old prescription: 'Live on sixpence a day and earn it'."[4]

Once he had caught the eye of the critics his confidence grew, especially with publishers like John Lane. Lane invited him to a crucial meeting with an American publisher whom he hoped would take his book of poems: "If you interest him, he'll take it; so I want you to be brilliant." Laurence agreed, in a fit of typically exuberant enthusiasm, adding, "All right, give me champagne and I will be." Lane agreed and Laurence charmed the American with his wit and humour. Afterwards Lane smiled with pleasure, "You were!" He praised Laurence's display of "brilliance", and the book was placed "to his satisfaction".

An inherent streak of egotism, especially

Title design for Edith Nesbit,
A Pomander of Verse, *1895.*

found it too difficult to be sincere about the poetry he thought weak and far inferior to her children's stories. The one time he relented and praised just one of her poems as an example of "good verse", she took the compliment as patronising: "That is the *first* time you have ever praised my poetry!" she told him in disgust. In the end he stopped visiting her and their relationship faded; for such erratic and trying behaviour would always alienate Laurence, however strong the ties of friendship.[5]

On the other hand Laurence was always his own fiercest critic. His judgement was damaged only by the pressure of work. In later years his opponents thought him too prolific and not self-critical enough. True, he had a restless creative talent, and tried to master as many of the creative arts as possible, from drawing, prose, poetry to journalism, drama, lectures as well as writing novels and stories. But in 1945 he declared of the sixty-five books he had written, just four stories he considered to be his best. The danger was too much versatility and not enough artistry, according to some critics. But Laurence disagreed

---

Frontispiece, "When Pan was Dead" and title design to All-Fellows, *1896.*

and was equally outspoken in his retort: "It is charged against me that I have been 'too versatile'; but how can anyone with gifts of expression, whom life really interests, avoid being versatile? Life is the most versatile thing under the sun; and in pursuit of life and character the author who works in a groove works in blinkers."[6] Only Alfred's calm, carefully considered, at times caustic criticism was taken seriously: "My brother used to say I wrote faster than he could read. He wrote two books of poems – better than all mine put together."[7]

Versatility led to renewed experiments with new books. Using his religious obsession, he planned a series of books which combined poetry and prose legends, based upon universal biblical themes like "The Truce of God" and "The Tree of Guile". The first was published as *All-Fellows. Seven Legends of Lower Redemption*, by Kegan Paul at the end of 1896. It appeared in time for the Christmas book lists and was reviewed alongside *Green Arras* in the book columns. Its mixture of religious sentiment, and seven firm-outline drawings in the spirit of Burne-Jones and Ricketts, made it a favourite with Laurence, who years later declared it "still has my heart". His only fear was that the pious nature of the subjects – which dealt with temptation

ALL-FELLOWS
SEVEN LEGENDS OF
LOWER REDEMPTION
WITH INSETS IN
VERSE BY LAURENCE HOUSMAN

LONDON: KEGAN PAUL, TRENCH, TRÜBNER AND CO., LIMITED, PATERNOSTER HOUSE, CHARING CROSS ROAD
1896

"The Truce of God", from
All-Fellows, *1896.*

"The Tree of Guile", from
All-Fellows, *1896.*

and evil – might alientate readers; "that an assault is meant on things which they hold sacred". This was not his intention. The drawings of elongated and distorted figures posed in a series of open doorways and windows were praised by Gleeson White as "some of his most matured illustrations"; others praised their qualities of "epicurean aestheticism". But the greatest satisfaction came from Oscar Wilde, who received the book with a copy of Alfred's *A Shropshire Lad*, and wrote to Laurence: "Thus, you and your brother have given me a few moments of that rare thing called happiness." It was a comforting confession from the fallen idol of their generation, who had recently emerged from prison. [8]

The appearance of *A Shropshire Lad* had a profound effect upon Laurence's literary ambitions as well. His brother's collection of sixty-three poems, published by Kegan Paul early in 1896, was a threat to his own bid for critical attention as a writer of verse. Laurence always remembered how it arrived "like a bolt from the blue...and straightaway as an author with

any individuality worth mentioning, I was wiped out. I became the brother of the 'Shropshire Lad'; and for the next five years I laboured under the shadow of that bright cloud." His only consolation, especially in later years, was the thought that Alfred's private life of loneliness and self-torture was "in general much less happy than my own". [9]

Nevertheless, two years passed before Laurence published another volume of poems. It was called *Spikenard. A Book of Devotional Love Poems*, and published by Alfred's friend Grant Richards in 1898. Although unillustrated, the cover design stamped in gold on brown paper boards was singled out by *The Studio* as "an ideally perfect example of restrained decoration to be placed among the first dozen modern bindings". The twenty-three devotional poems were subjects which "would supply a religious painter with inspiring themes", according to *The Studio*; although Alfred dismissed them as largely "nonsense themes". The title alone suggested his aesthetic preoccupations of the period; used the exoticism of the eastern plant, spikenard, and combined Laurence's passion for the atmospheric, the obscure alongside the commonplace. The book also marked his brief relationship with its publisher, the young Grant Richards, who published his next book of verse as well. Called *The Little Land, with Songs from its Four Rivers*, it appeared in 1899, illustrated with slight though quite individual line drawings of classical winged figures engraved in clear outline by Clemence.

Poetry was the inspiration for the next series of drawings, which he considered "the best drawings I ever did". Although it was not his own verse, he greatly admired Shelley's poem *The Sensitive Plant*, the story of a poet's spirit seen as the sensitive plant, growing in an idyllic garden tended by a beautiful woman – the symbol of true beauty. The tale appealed to his own search for spiritual ideals in the face of worldly temptations and corruption. For when the beautiful woman dies, death and corruption settle over the garden, and Shelley asks whether seeing beauty is a permanent experience; if so, it is life which is not real.

Describing why he chose to illustrate the poem, in his preface Laurence explained it was "too absolute" to properly illustrate, but offered certain symbolic challenges which appealed to his own love of visual imagery. He sought an "appreciation, an individual sense of delight or emotion in a work of finished and constructive beauty". The search for beauty in the world was a favourite preoccupation of his own generation: "Man's sense of beauty is his own: it is not Nature's. The aim of all art is to restrict Nature, and teach her that her place is not in the high places of men; and we only admire Nature because in the present strength of our civilization we are strong enough to pet her." But his drawings to the poem were limited by what he saw as a constantly changing ideal of beauty; eventually he hoped the world would abandon the search.

The twelve full-page drawings and initial letters he produced for process engraving

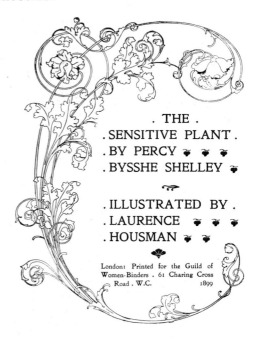

Title design for The Sensitive Plant, *1898.*

are among his most carefully considered, delicate and successful ink drawings. Having been asked to illustrate a favourite poem for a series of illustrated poems edited by Ernst Rhys for Aldine House, he accepted lower terms and a smaller royalty for the work, (although the publisher later refused his royalties). But the sympathetic theme of the poem, the opportunity to develop his favourite garden themes and atmospheric settings, helped him to create "something technically in advance of anything I had previously done"; and at first the publisher "was rapturous in his appreciation". The drawings are remarkably detailed, their fine etched line surfaces and intricate stipple work shading recall the best of Millais and Rossetti. He mastered the sense of mystery with statuesque classical figures set amongst flowers and foliage which, according to one admirer, avoided the dangerous pitfall of his predecessors' "invincible quaintness". The elongated figures with firm classical lines

Opposite and overleaf: Ten illustrations to Shelley's The Sensitive Plant, *1898.*

suggested Moreau as much as Greek or Roman statuary; their limbs extended as if "an image of the spirit's importance in comparison with the body".[10] But the key to their success was in the garden settings, where beauty survived unharmed in "the exquisite ministrations, the sounds, and fragrance and sweet winds of the garden enclosed". This was the ideal world of Laurence's dream, "the perfect ensemble of the garden, its sunny lawns and rose-trellises, its fountains, statues, and flower-scented ways; realised, too, the spirit of the Sensitive Plant, the lady of the garden, and Pan the great god who never dies, who waits only without the garden, till in a little while he enters, 'effacing and replacing with his own image and superscription, the parenthetic grace...of the garden deity'."[11]

* * * * * * * * * * * *

Eloquence and passionate declarations of belief were the mark of Laurence the art critic and journalist as well. Ever since his first article defended Blake as an impressionist, he adopted a crusading tone when writing about those neglected artists he admired. He wrote an influential and perceptive analysis of Arthur Boyd Houghton for the *Bibliographica* in 1895, which set out to reinstate this unjustly neglected master of black-and-white, whom *The Studio* called a Victorian hack devoted to "the glorification of the crinoline". He strengthened his crusade by publishing a selection of Houghton's drawings and wood engravings, with a perceptive essay which drew on his own experiences drawing for wood engraving. *The Studio* gave this volume generous coverage, although it was somewhat dismissive of Laurence's intentions in this "age of resurrections". Their conclusion was that "the present revival of the cultus of Arthur Boyd Houghton is mainly due to the passionate advocacy of Mr Laurence Housman".

Laurence was especially concerned with fluctuations in popular taste. Those passages in his autobiography concerning the ugliness of Bromsgrove's interiors of a past age, proved how much his taste had changed once he left home for London. His art school training forced him to prepare to pander to a public's fickle taste in decorative design – a subject he later used to declare a nation's responsibility was to prepare its aspiring art students and the public with artistic standards of permanence and quality. Moreover, he began his essay about Donatello's sculpture (which had now also suffered from public disfavour) with the perceptive observation: "Perhaps the most perfect proof of great artistic form is to be found in the serenity with which it survives the period of its innovating force. Posterity's acceptance of what genius has imposed tends to make the originality marked when once the formula of a new style has attained securely to classical rank."[12]

His was a voice of concern in an age when novelty took precedence over artistic quality. He became a spokesman for neglected heroes of the past, for the Victorian artist's preoccupation with detail in nature, for literary puzzles, symbolism, historical and mythological models applied to his own search for beauty and religious ideals. He was a devoted Victorian, "one of the last of that breed", one obituary writer labelled him. And yet his associations with the Nineties figures, like Beardsley, Wilde and Lane, often overshadowed his singular crusades for selected past values. Not that this new generation lacked values; he admired the spontaneous and the individual, for these had spawned some of the greatest of his heroes' works. "For God's sake let us use our eyes, and trust to our feelings. Don't let us shut our eyes, or bandage them in grandmotherly traditions," he pleaded in defence of his beloved Pre-Raphaelites.[13] He saw them alone as true innovators, creators of a new individualism who brought to romantic art "the ideal in terms of reality". They founded "a new school of quality, sincere, human, and intense, which art had never attained before". They were liberators from the prison of outmoded traditions and their present disciples, like Ricketts, the Society of Twelve and the New English Art Club – which turned its back on academic traditions – were "the youthful experimentors who now hark back to the last period of authentic inspiration in British Art". They were "nearer to its spirit than those who have but carried with them its reminiscences into age".[14]

Laurence's great skill as a journalist was an ability to convince his readers in simple, clear language, using precise examples. His love of the Pre-Raphaelite rebellion led to his address, "Pre-Raphaelitism in Art and Poetry", for the 1928 Rossetti centenary celebrations. It remains "one of the most balanced appraisals that has been made of the movement" according to Fredeman; and centred around a simple metaphor: "Art was a coffin in which Raphael lay embalmed. Therefore, in order not to remain mutes at a funeral, the men of the new movement had to become Pre-Raphaelites; get rid, not of the living Raphael, but of his corpse. First and foremost they had to find themselves."[15]

Much of this clarity and crusading had arisen out of the sixteen years he spent as art critic for the *Manchester Guardian*. He was given the position in 1895, on the strength of his confident Arthur Boyd Houghton essay, and the fact that he had begun to establish himself as an artist. The appointment meant he reviewed current exhibitions in London and wrote about the state of artistic taste in the country. At first he accepted the position for the financial security it offered, still unable to earn enough from drawing and writing: "Not only did it relieve me during the first five years, from the fear of starvation, but it gave me confidence and a power of ready writing which till then I had lacked. Hitherto I had waited too much upon mood, and when dissatisfied with results would often put away a piece of writing and not look at it again for months – sometimes indeed, never." This new-found sense of power in his role as art critic, might have made him more egotistical; instead he always dismissed his Guardian work as "pot-boiling". Those steady rounds of recent exhibitions he saw as his education, "a corrective in things contemporary" which forced him to look further than the Pre-Raphaelite obsessions of Rossetti's medievalism, and the Sixties School.

Eventually the sheer monotony of un-ending deadlines, writing within very limited space and the pressure of writing to order, (sometimes wiring his reviews to Manchester within the same night as the Private View), took its toll. He was forced to learn brevity and to analyse at a moment's notice. He dreaded the annual survey of the year's pictures which was to fill just two pages; and he long remembered the time he was told to write three columns on "History of Art in Europe in the last Hundred Years" to fill a last minute hole on one page - to be finished within twenty-four hours. He always felt uncomfortable at Private Views, when his sense of inexpe-rience, which never left him, and a fatal respect for his powerful position, forced him to the edge of a room to make way for his more distinguished critic colleagues. From this viewpoint he watched these pompous critics with their disciples in tow, and decided "humanity became an amusing study" when he should have been studying the pictures. "Some of the 'authorities' (one especially) I sedulously avoided; others were kindly patronizing, without too much insistence upon submissive agree-ment." He was plagued by recurring doubts: "Was I right to take a position which at least gave me a certain amount of influence over the reputations and market-value of men who knew so much more about painting than I did?" In the end, he took comfort in his own love of painting; although this too was undermined by the fact he never actually tried to paint himself. "My qualifications were of the slenderest kind; my own practice was entirely in black-and -white, and only line-work at that. I did not know how to paint; I did not want to paint; about the technique of painting I knew almost nothing; I still do not," he remembered in his autobiography. But the critic had to be opinionated, and here he was well qualified; armed with "strong likes and dislikes with which I was prob-ably able to infect a proportion of my readers". And in the end he was thankful for the chance to practice his writing, "to write better, and certainly to write more, of the things I wished to write than would otherwise have been possible".

His editor praised his abilities; and when, in 1900, he tried to resign he was offered a new contract, "on very generous terms, asking me to undertake at a raised fee the bigger shows of the year; while for the smaller ones he provided an understudy from his London staff". When he did resign in 1914, his motives were personal. He could not accept the job of "enabling pictures to become a market commodity, and attract purchasers"; or at worst "help people at social gatherings to talk semi-intelligently about the pictures of the year and fancy themselves art-lovers" when the country was at war. And yet over the years he had been the spur to many heated controversies; writing with "force and wit" to damn the purchase of an inferior Holman Hunt picture for the National Gallery; or to fan the flames of outrage over Jacob Epstein's exuberant and daring nude sculptures for the British Medical Association building.[16]

Tailpiece from Goblin Market, *1893.*

Jump to Glory Jane, *1892*.

Drawing To a Close

hroughout the late 1890s, Laurence continued to provide occasional book designs for various publishers, alternating the work with illustrations, reviews for the Guardian, poetry and articles for numerous magazines. The amount of concentrated effort involved in even the slightest cover or title page design meant he managed to accomplish a surprising amount in four or five years.

Several new publishers commissioned book designs of special note, including a cover and title-page for George Knight's short story collection, *Dust in the Balance*, 1896, for Jarrold & Sons; followed by a cover and title vignette for the same publisher's edition of George Morley's *Sweet Audrey*, 1899. Grant Richards commissioned a cover design for Alice Meynell's poetry anthology, *The Flower of the Mind*, 1896; and Archibald Constable commissioned a title-page for editions of George Meredith's *Selected Poems*,

Initial letters designed by Housman.

and for Meredith's *Nature Poems*, both published in 1898. Otherwise John Lane managed to secure most of his time, with a major new series of designs for cover, title and tailpiece to Edmond Holme's *The Silence of Love*, 1899, for which Laurence planned a striking, large-format volume, bound in blue with a triangular floral motif on the cover and art nouveau interlace on the title-page. Lane was so pleased with the designs he re-used the cover motif on a later edition of *Walt Whitman's Poetry*, 1902.

Indeed, Laurence had developed a high reputation as a binding designer by the end of the century, his designs often linked with Ricketts and members of the burgeoning fine printing revival. The rich ornamental gilt pattern on blue cloth he devised for H.C.Marillier's *Dante Gabriel Rossetti: An Illustrated Memorial of his Life and Work*, published by George Bell in 1899, brought lavish praises from *The Studio* book binding critic, Esther Wood. She felt the design "fulfills its decorative purpose with dignity and charm. It belongs to the successes of pure ornament; rich in conception, stongly composed, and congruous with the temperament of the author."[1]

Kegan Paul continued to commission work, most notably the series of spare line drawings engraved by Clemence for an edition of Thomas à Kempis's *Of the Imitation of Christ,* in 1899. These confident architectural drawings are unique to Laurence's *oeuvre.* They employ a knowledge of Renaissance architecture, which had also inspired his nearest rival Ricketts,

Cover design by Housman to H.C.Marillier's
Dante Gabriel Rossetti, *1899.*

but here used to contrast with the gaunt, exaggerated figure of Christ. In a sense it was an exercise in geometric symmetry: the classical severity of arches, domes and erect mock-corinthian columns broken only by some rather daring diagonals and the sinewy limbs and compressed drapery drawn in an altogether freer style. The

commission was followed by an elaborate floral border design used on the title-page for Kegan Paul's anthology of his own writings, *On the Way Side, Verse and Translations*, published in 1899; as well as a title-page for his newest editorial venture, *The English Bookman's Library*, in 1899.

For many of his illustration commissions Laurence insisted upon drawing for wood engravings – these preferably engraved by Clemence. On those occasions when his work was photoengraved, it was usually done to preserve the delicacy of his pastel shading ("Green Gaffer"), or the purity of his pen line (*Sensitive Plant*). The photo-engraving process in fact eventually destroyed the wood engraving profession with its faster, cheaper methods and the ability to reproduce the subtlety of wash or pencil which took the wood engraver more time to transpose into line. By the turn of the century then, a large number of Laurence's drawings were photoengraved, such as his frontispiece to John White-Rodyng's collection of nine plays, *The Night*, in 1900. This was published by Beardsley's friend and publisher, Leonard Smithers. Laurence was clearly aware of the connection when he took on the project, and he wrote Smithers to suggest "a page size like [Beardsley's] Salomé would best suit the drawing".[2] His love for Arthur Hughes' illustrations continued; and he even made a new frontispiece and cover design for a reissue of Hughes's illustrated edition of George Macdonald's classic tale, *At the Back of the North Wind*, 1900, which was successful enough to be re-used in subsequent new editions of Macdonald's tales (see appendix).

Although primarily a book designer and illustrator, Laurence had, over the years, contributed various drawings to magazines as well. By the 1890s a number of new fine art journals had appeared; those artistic quarterlies or annuals intended to appeal to a select, aesthetically aware readership. Priced at six shillings or a guinea, they were expensive examples of fine printing and production. *The Yellow Book* was perhaps the most notorious, and Laurence's associations with it, from the first issue in 1894, must have encouraged his belief in the value of such ventures. They helped to support many young illustrators and writers as well as to expose this new talent to a wider, yet discriminating public.

Another influential but short-lived fine art and literary magazine was *The Pageant*, a short-lived annual which lasted from 1896-97, under the editorship of Gleeson White and Charles Shannon. Here appeared some of the most impressive names of art and literature: the drawings of Rossetti,

Whistler, Ricketts, a few by Laurence published alongside articles and poems by Swinburne, Yeats, Verlaine and John Gray. Laurence's contributions were in fact stories as well as the rather dubious pen drawing "Death and the Bather", which appeared in the first number in 1896. This was an elaborate grouping of male nudes bathing in a stream, and was clearly a symbolic work of the kind John Lane often censored. Here too were shades of Beardsley's own elongated nude illustrations, but drawn in a refined figure style less dependent upon pure outline. The nudity and the suggestiveness of these poses must have raised a few eyebrows; if only for the convoluted grouping of long male limbs and exaggerated heads which he seemed to pile one atop the other in a flagrant disregard for the conventional laws of perspective. His second drawing, "The Invisible Princess", appeared in 1897, and was more successful. Its medieval subject and firm outline style was a homage to Dürer; yet the composition of a young man embracing an invisible woman in the tower is full of stark contrasts between heavy shading and the light, dream-like space of an imaginary medieval city (see illustration in Chapter 4).

As the number of these magazines increased, their editors borrowed contributors and tried to secure designs from the most influential and popular artists. The publisher of *The Pageant* was Henry & Co., and following its failure, the firm promoted another annual, this time intended to appeal to the juvenile market. *The Parade: An Illustrated Gift Book for Boys and Girls* appeared once, in 1897, with a title page designed by Beardsley and cover and endpapers by Paul Woodroffe. Laurence contributed a fairy-tale drawing, "An Enchanted Princess", and this appeared alongside articles and poems by such "celebrated names" as Richard Le Gallienne and Max Beerbohm, although they were perhaps too rarefied for such young readers.

The key to the success of these new magazines lay in fine printing and quality production as well. As John Lane discovered, presentation could sell even the most obscure book of poems. Unfortunately not every new magazine venture to which Laurence contributed realised this. Even the most ambitious editors or lavish productions were often doomed to fail. For example, *The Windmill* was an illustrated quarterly which lasted one issue (October 1898). Laurence contributed a poem, "A Sonnet", and a brief sketch "Marionettes", which was more experimental than finished. But the drawing was poorly printed and critics seemed to think such carelessness suggested the overall failure of the magazine to understand its market. *The Star* critic savaged the first issue, where "various tailpieces have the musty savour of the stock horrors of a jobbing printer". Then he turned to attack Laurence's drawing,

"Death and the Bather", from
The Pageant, *1896.*

which was reproduced as a typical example: "To enable our readers to judge for themselves as to the sorry rubbish shot into this imposing 'quarterly', we reproduce by photography, same size, what Mr Laurence Housman is pleased to call 'Marionettes' which look as if they had been scratched with a bad pen by a blind man."

Among his more successful contributions were those which appeared in *The Dome*, a shilling quarterly founded in March 1897. Laurence's stories and articles appeared in eight issues, while three further issues contained his drawings as well. It was a successful association with a much admired and well-printed magazine, which soon was so successful it changed from quarterly to monthly publication on the strength of its influence. Divided into sections devoted to Architecture, Literature, Drawing, Painting, Engraving and

Music, *The Dome* sought to present "Examples of all the Arts". Here Laurence's drawings were given prominence as full page engravings; the last, "Cauchemar" was even printed on pure linen paper. His illustrated story, "The Troubling of the Waters" appeared in the second issue with the drawing as a frontispiece. It was a powerful Cain and Abel tale, which was later praised for its "strength and violence ...the illustration might pass with the most observant for a woodblock of the best of the 'sixties'. In its nervous strength and passion it recalls Sandys."[3] Then followed the stark, atmospheric drawing, "The Well at the Wall", with its carefully composed composition of off-centre archways and hooded monks, again highly praised as an "exquisite piece of architectural drawing". On the whole, *The Dome* was an important new venture which associated Laurence with a new generation of private press illustrators, fine printers and engravers. His drawings here appeared alongside the woodcuts and engravings of such noted figures as Gordon Craig, William Nicholson, Bernard Sleigh, J.T.Guthrie and Byam Shaw, as well as the etchings of William Strang and portrait lithographs of his friend William Rothenstein. Here too Clemence engraved briefly after drawings by Philip Connard. And, as a literary venue, *The Dome* first published Laurence's most delightful fairy-tale, "A Capful of Moonshine", in the October 1898 issue. Occasionally its editors reviewed his latest books as well.

The stirring success of *The Dome* must have had a considerable influence on Laurence's decision to start his own magazine. Enviously he had watched other successes; he had seen Ricketts and Shannon pour all their energies into *The Dial*, and played a minor role in the birth of *The Yellow Book*. Charged with enthusiasm for his own venture, he secured the editorial assistance of Somerset Maugham and together they produced the first issue of *The Venture. An Annual of Art and Literature*, in the autumn of 1903. Laurence insisted upon quality production and fine printing, and he employed J.T.Guthrie at the Pear Tree Press as his printer. He poached several literary and artistic contributors from *The Dome*, and filled the first weighty volume of 249 pages with engravings and drawings by Ricketts and Shannon, T.Sturge Moore, Gordon Craig, Bernard Sleigh and Lucien Pissarro, as well as poems, stories and articles by the more established literary figures like Thomas Hardy, John Masefield, G.K.Chesterton. He even appealed successfully for contributions from John Lane's authors Francis Thompson, John Gray and Alice Meynell. There was a strong Housman content as well: Laurence had secured a poem from his brother Alfred, as well as contributing his own story, "Proverbial Romances". Each contributor was told from the start there would be no payment for their work, only a share in the profits, if there were any. But gradually Laurence's publishing inexperience overshadowed his plans. Later he decided "the whole thing was, of course, too highbrow to be popular"; he should have aimed at a more select market by pricing *The Venture* at a guinea instead of five shillings. He clearly wanted a success; even when he later recalled the upset of failure, he remained unrepentent: "I think it deserved to be". The critics generally agreed: some praised its "manly type and strong line drawings"; while *The Studio* wished it "a long life...there is room for a magazine for the encouragement of artistic effort which by its virtuosity is suited for the uses of popular journalism". But *The Venture* was truly a short-lived dream, which faded away after the first issue.

Through her brother's associations with editors and printers, Clemence was employed as an engraver for these various new fine printing projects. Now that her engravings for Roberts had finally dried up, her main source of income came from engraving after Laurence's drawings and for James Guthrie's Pear Tree Press, as well as occasional work for C.R.Ashbee's Essex House Press. Together she and Laurence learnt from both these artist-printers the luxury of working outside the traumatic world of commercial publishing. Here time and patience was rewarded with superb printing of their work, often on fine paper and elegantly bound for the collector market. Together they produced an edition of Tennyson's *Maud* which Ashbee printed in 1905 in an edition of 125 copies. Laurence drew the frontispiece illustration of a young girl beside a stream, Reginald Savage transferred it to the wood block, and Clemence engraved it. The result, bound in a fine white vellum binding with a stamped rose and "Soul is form" on the cover, is a triumph of the new era of Arts and Crafts printing.

From such collaborations, James Guthrie was a devoted admirer of Clemence's engraving skill and he soon became her greatest disciple. On the other hand, she pronounced his incredibly intricate drawings of dense foliage and complex landscapes too detailed for her graver, although she succeeded remarkably well. The British Museum owns a series of these landscape engravings, among them the superb "Evening Star" which, in its subtle mastery of form within the masses of tight, compact foliage, must be one of Clemence's most successful engravings. It was such work which led Guthrie to conclude: "Her blocks are not only a marvel of faith, but a marvel of sympathy." He claimed no English engraving collection should be without one of her engraved proofs – which were rare enough since she refused to use a press and took her own burnished proofs. "In technical range no engraver has carried the art further, except perhaps in the evaporation of lineal form in tones, which is aside from this still waiting a modern exponent."[4]

Laurence's illustrations and Clemence's engravings attracted serious students of a younger generation as well. The most famous was Paul Woodroffe, a budding young artist whose work appeared alongside Laurence's in *The Quarto* and *The Parade*. Although a devoted disciple at first of Walter Crane's stylised, firm medieval outline style, which influenced his own first book, *Ye Booke of Nursery Rhymes* in 1895, gradually Woodroffe came under the more expressive, delicate detailed style of Housman. When they met they discovered a common passion for the Sixties School illustrators, as well as medieval tales of romance, religion and adventure. This led to the collaboration volume, *The Confessions of St Augustine*, which Kegan Paul agreed to publish in 1900. Laurence provided a title page design, Woodroffe drew the illustrations and Clemence engraved them on wood.

A favourite medieval tale was the thirteenth century French love story, *Of Aucassin and Nicolette*, for which Woodroffe had drawn his own illustrations. It had been fifteen years since the story appeared in English translation by Laurence's neighbour, Andrew Lang. And so, on the strength of Woodroffe's illustrations, the publisher John Murray asked Laurence to provide a "free translation" to fit these drawings, which Clemence again agreed to engrave, and the book appeared late in 1902. *The Studio* gave the project full coverage, although the emphasis fell on Clemence's engravings rather than Laurence's translation: "Mr Housman has given an extremely free rendering, näively explaining that the liberties he has taken were necessitated by the fact that the illustrations were done in advance by Mr Woodroffe, and the translation was made to suit them! This would, of course, be a dangerous precedent to follow, but the beauty of the drawings is so great, and they have been so exquisitely engraved by Miss Clemence Housman, that every true lover of art must condone the offense against literary accuracy." But it was the last of the Woodroffe-Housman collaborations, and although the artist went on to perpetuate Laurence's love of intricate background detail and exaggerated figure expressions, and to emulate his distinctive bindings, he eventually turned to stained glass design. In the end, he was overshadowed by his mentor, and until recently dismissed as a "rather second-hand" artist of the book.[5] But he remains an important link between Housman and a future generation of artists of the illustrated book.

Shades of Oscar

ith his enchanting wit and generous, sympathetic nature, Laurence was popular with the young as well as the more established literary and artistic figures of his day. He was readily accepted in the artistic circle of the Nineties, noted for its eccentricity and influence, which had its base in the Café Royal. Here he remained the youngest of his literary friends, who included George Bernard Shaw and Frank Harris. He frequently escaped the tedium of work in Kensington, or the noise of Piccadilly after a meeting with John Lane, for the chance to chat with them in the smoke-filled splendour of the café. Laurence's friend Max Beerbohm best described the intoxicating atmosphere as he entered that "exuberant vista of gilding and crimson velvet set amidst all those opposing mirrors and upholding caryatids, with fumes of tobacco ever rising to the painted and pagan ceiling, and with the hum of presumeably cynical conversation broken into so sharply now and again by the clatter of dominoes shuffled on marble tables". Like Laurence, Max had first arrived a starry-eyed youth, and was immediately captivated: "I drew a deep breath and 'This indeed,' said I to myself, 'is life!' "[1]

Over the years Laurence frequently met his friends and publishers here, and entertained them when he had the money. He was a striking figure, as his friend and fellow café visitor William Rothenstein best conveyed in two rare portrait drawings. They were done in 1898, for his *Liber Studiorum*, and depict a handsome, gentle-looking man of thirty-three, with a rather solid bearing, a square head of thick dark hair and the carefully trimmed beard he kept until his death. He was seated, wearing a generously cut jacket, wing collar and tie; a model of respectability. Only his expression is tempered by an intense, if vacant stare; which suggests either boredom or his greater probing nature.

Another frequenter of the café was the publisher Grant Richards, whom Laurence had met there with his brother Alfred. Richards was at the time rather hard-pressed financially; but he was an enterprising new publisher always in search of literary talent. He was apparently in awe of Laurence's literary reputation and his numerous famous friends at the time, and described him as "a person whose goodwill counted in the commonwealth of letters". But from the first meeting their relationship grew, and Richards published Laurence's poetry as well as revelled in his charm and wit. On one memorable occasion Laurence challenged Richards that he could not produce a meal of hedgehogs at a London restaurant within twenty four hours. Richards took the bet, and although he could ill afford it, produced the promised animals which came from Scotland. They dined together, amid much merriment on a prolonged and lavish meal of several courses and wines, which left Richards considerably poorer but nevertheless en-

Laurence Housman in 1898, by
William Rothenstein
Lithographic chalk, 8⅞ x 6⅜",
British Library.

chanted by Laurence's bizarre sense of fun.

Laurence was generally a sociable being who delighted in such adventures. But he quickly grew intolerant of pretence or forced egotism. Once, while visiting Ricketts at The Vale, the famous Whistler arrived in a fierce temper, "full of flatulence" of the supposed outrage his disciple

Walter Sickert had committed against him. Laurence and the other guests were expected to sit quietly and give Whistler their complete attention. He repeated the same monotonous charge over and over, until Laurence could stand it no longer. He asked to see a Ricketts drawing for *The Pageant*, to escape the strained atmosphere, "when the tedium of it became too much for me"; and then quickly left

One of Housman's several evocative male nudes, "McNoonie in the Sleeping Palace", from A Farm in Fairyland, *1894.*

[98]

the house. The evening had been "a nightmare" he concluded; and it enhanced his belief that "great men are not always nice or even interesting to meet".[2]

There was a youthfulness in Laurence's character, even in middle age, which attracted him to the young. This made acceptance of his own homosexuality that much easier – unlike his brother Alfred, who was tormented by an ill-fated love for his Oxford friend and London companion, Moses Jackson, (who eventually married and moved to India). In the end Alfred could never quite accept his true nature. Laurence, on the other hand, delighted in the eccentricities and occasional bouts of outrageous behaviour his young, more liberated friends devised for his entertainment. His verses and drawings were done in this spirit, and they could be interpreted as expressions of his longing for a loving friend – especially constant references to his search for true love. One critic shrewdly noted he made more drawings of young nude men than of women, which was certainly true. As time passed, and Laurence saw the importance of accepting his nature, he befriended Oscar Wilde, who became his new mentor. Later still, he became an outspoken champion of sexual freedom and attacked public discrimination by writing articles ("The Relation of Fellow-Feeling to Sex"), and lecturing on the subject to numerous groups.

He shared this love of outrageous behaviour with his closest friend and companion, the young painter Herbert Alexander. Herbert, or "Sandro" as Laurence called him, was nine years Laurence's junior, a London-born artist largely self-taught, with only brief training at the Herkomer School and the Slade. He was a delightful, sensitive yet comical character who endeared himself to Laurence during his own early days in London. They were rarely apart, shared mutual interests in painting as well as a schoolboy love of practical jokes and schemes to shock Herbert's parents. On summer holidays together they went bicycling, tenting or sunbathed, and Laurence occasionally visited Herbert's family home. There, from the start, Laurence felt inferior; a poor artist with a torn lining in his jacket, who refused to surrender it to the

servant at the door for fear of detection – he kept it under his mattress instead. But Herbert inspired his confidence and their schemes to shock the family were hugely successful. Once Laurence appeared for dinner dressed in a scanty Greek tunic to compliment Herbert's "Cupid" costume. On another occasion Herbert's father was outraged to discover Laurence, Herbert and some of their eccentric friends posing naked in a tree, for photographs they described as views of "arboreal men".

Herbert's paintings were highly detailed, serene landscapes and delicate floral compositions which delighted Laurence for their blatant disregard of popular taste and fashion. Laurence watched his friend's work improve under his influence, and that of his beloved Pre-Raphaelites. Later he claimed Herbert was "an artist, who, though still young and of barely matured power, has for a number of years been steadily developing a style of his own, little affected by outside influences". He wrote this in an article, praising "the quiet courage of his work" which he felt had skilfully avoided the dangerous "sentimentality of ruins" in landscapes of such picturesque subjects. And, in the autumn of 1899, as Laurence prepared to end his artistic career, he took Herbert to Italy in search of new landscape subjects, while he sent home vivid descriptions of their journey to his mother and to Clemence. Under Laurence's sympathetic guidance Herbert eventually attained a moderate success as a painter: he was elected an associate of the RWS in 1905 and a full member in 1927.[3]

As a prelude to their Italian excursion, Laurence took Herbert with him on an "errand of mercy" to meet the exiled Oscar Wilde in Paris. His Café Royal friends had taken up a collection on Wilde's behalf, following news that he was in debt to his landlord. Since Laurence was known as "the youngest", they instructed him to go to Paris, to give no money to Wilde but pay off his debts. Laurence agreed not knowing the visit would prove one of the most important to his life and future ambitions. From the early news that Wilde had admired his Green Gaffer, Laurence shared with Alfred a sense of admiration and "oneness" with Wilde. Despite his recent downfall, imprisonment, and now his tragic exile in Paris, under the assumed name of Sebastian Melmouth, Laurence continued to admire Wilde. It was in fact the first of several such meetings between Laurence and Wilde, which later inspired his book, *Echo de Paris: a Study from Life,* 1923. This was a record of their conversations, and a reading of these provides a rare glimpse of Laurence's own private nature and his changing attitudes toward art and the role of the artist in society.

Before their first meeting, Laurence's friendship with Wilde had been through letters, which he wrote like a humble disciple writing to his master. Laurence shared the sense of outrage at Wilde's two year imprisonment in 1895, but as a sympathetic fellow artist and writer, he was not one of the scandalized public who believed Wilde's downfall marked the end of an artistic era — certainly not the end of decadence and immorality as some believed. As one historian of the period noted: "Dandy of intellect, dandy of manners, dandy of dress, Oscar Wilde strutted through the first half of the Nineties and staggered through the last."[4] Indeed, since his imprisonment, Wilde had become even more of a heroic figure to Laurence. He had encouraged his descriptive abilities and once asked him: "And when, pray, are we to have another work from your pen?". His poems had given Wilde "that rare thing — happiness", and following this news, Laurence wrote a long, friendly letter and their friendship blossomed. He received an affectionate personal reply from Wilde just before Christmas (14 December 1898) the year previous to their meeting him in Paris. In it he thanked Laurence for his kind letters and added, "Style is certainly part of your character: your soul has beautiful curves and colours". Laurence had expressed concern over Wilde's welfare, but was reassured he was well enough, and even planned a month holiday near Cannes, "at the end of which I am to produce a work of art: I hope I shall be able to do something. The high sapphire wall of sea, the gold dust of the sun, the petals and perfumes of Southern flowers – perhaps these may tune my soul to some note of beauty."[5]

When Laurence and Herbert arrived in Paris they were greeted by Wilde's friend, Robert Ross, and taken to the café where Wilde met them. Laurence was first shocked by Wilde's pallid, pathetic appearance, but as the conversation turned to art "for a moment at least he was back at his old form again". Laurence remembered his remarks well enough to publish them years later as the poignant and inspiring confessions of a failed but heroic artist. He saw them as the record of failure, and "failures interest me more, generally, than success. If I am asked why, my answer is that they seem to reveal human nature more truly, and, on the whole, more encouragingly, than anything else in the world. The way a man faces failure is the best proof of him." Wilde soon proved "the most accomplished talker I had ever met", especially on subjects of mutual interest like the search for beauty, form, style, or the role of the artist: "The greatest work of the imagination, for an artist, is to create first himself, then his public." Wilde was emphatic on the painful subject of success: "The artist's mission is to live the complete life: success, as an episode (which is all it can be); failure as the real, the final end...the highest function of the artist is to make perceived the beauty of failure."

Laurence turned to more personal matters, and asked why Wilde had liked his *Green Arras* poems. He replied with an air of self-confession, "Yours interested me — shall I confess? — partly because a few years ago it would have interested me so much less. For at that time, believing that I had discovered — that, in a way, I represented the symbol of my age, I was only interested in myself. Now, in an age to which I do not belong, I find myself interested in others."[6]

There was an open frankness about his remarks which appealed to Laurence. His courage was an object lesson; his obvious suffering Laurence believed the result of a gross injustice to personal freedom. This, above all, was pathetic yet inspiring: "But what I admired most was the quiet, uncomplaining courage with which he accepted an ostracism against which, in his lifetime, there could be no appeal. To a man of his habits and temperament...the outlook was utterly dark: life had already become a tomb." He added a footnote in *Echo de Paris* (which he reprinted in a later anthology of writings, *Backwards and Forewards*, 1945) to re-emphasize the injustices Wilde had suffered and praise his courage for making "the 'unmentionable' mentionable": "What a strange irony of life, that the man who tried most to detach himself from the unlovely complications of modern civilization should have become the symbol, or the byword, of one of its least-solved problems; and that patience or the charity to trace to its origin, should have supplied him so savagely with that 'complete life of the artist' which successes could never have given him." By then Laurence had accepted his own "true nature" and begun to campaign for public acceptance of the "unmentionable" side of Wilde's life.

At the end of their first meeting, a surprise visitor had been planned, who Wilde had not seen for "three disintegrated years". Laurence tried to keep Wilde busy while they waited, but in the end it was no use. The friend had seen Wilde and not wanting to be recognised, left promptly: "The savour had gone from the meeting. Wilde excused himself and left them."[7] It was a sad end to a deeply emotional experience for Laurence. But the lessons Wilde taught him were not wasted; they inspired his own ambitions to pursue a career of wider scope and ambition when he returned to London.

* * * * * * * * * * * *

When Laurence returned from the Continent, late in 1899, he neared the end of his artistic career. More time was spent over the next few months perfecting his literary skills, as he composed what would become his most popular book, *An Englishwoman's Love-Letters*. The story of this sensational "literary hoax" is given in the critic chapter below. Here one can mention that part of this book of fictional love letters was most probably inspired by Laurence's own letters home to his mother and Clemence, written while he was in Italy with Herbert, and he wrote the travel passages while they were still fresh in his mind. The book was published by John Murray late in 1900, and as early as the first week it sold out. Critics praised its poignancy, and readers of romantic fiction forced sales to enormous levels, until Laurence earned as much as £2,000 from this one book alone. Its success allowed him for the first time to enjoy the prospect of financial independence; as early as 8 January 1901, he confidently confessed to a friend, "fortune has begun to smile on me". He planned to return to the continent for "the whole of next winter", and to spend "some months of it in Capri", where he hoped to take a house. "I want to come with my sister and one friend, a man — two bedrooms and two sitting rooms would be sufficient and room for one servant besides," he explained.[8]

The success of this book also allowed him to take Clemence from Kensington to Battersea, where they took a flat at 70 York Mansions overlooking Battersea Park. On a clear day they could see across the river and all the way up to the "heights of Hampstead". But the restrictions of flat living soon wore thin, and within two years they moved back to Kensington. This time they chose the peaceful garden setting of Edwarde's Square, just off the bustling High Street, and found a house, 1 Pembroke Cottage, on the edge of the Georgian square. Their new home was opposite a pub, and here again they revelled in watching the fights and noisy crowds – this time of late drinkers at clearing out time on a Saturday evening – all from behind the safety of their own windows.

It was at this time Laurence tried to resign his Guardian post, but his editor persuaded him to stay on at a larger salary. He also managed more book designs, but the need to earn money now seemed less pressing, and he began to reconsider his career as an artist. Moreover, the most alarming new development was his poor eyesight, which had slowly been weakened by the intricate detail work he incorporated in his drawings. After nearly ten years drawing without a magnifying glass, his eyes had begun to fail. In the end, he accepted this unavoidable fact with good humour, buoyed by the prospect of his future as an author. And so, in October 1901, he sent the remains of his studio – some eighty-two ink drawings and sketches for *Goblin Market, All-Fellows, A Field of Clover,* and *The End of Elfin-Town* – to the Fine Art Society for his first one man exhibition. He recalled how "in the event the show was rather a farewell to illustration partly because I had found that I was more naturally cut out to be an author than an illustrator". His fellow critics turned up at the Private View and their notices, "as far as I remember were fairly kind," Laurence recalled; especially *The Studio* critic who devoted a full column to his review. Two years later Laurence was persuaded to exhibit once again, this time with engravings and woodcuts by Clemence and her fellow artist Louise Glazier at the newly opened John Baillie Gallery in nearby Bayswater. It was an experimental show in a gallery soon to become popular for its "Neglected Artists" exhibitions (which included Herbert Alexander's paintings a few years later). Laurence designed the invitation card to the Private View which contained the somewhat ominous drawing, "Give the Devil his Due", and the show in June 1902 was again a success.

Following his studio clear-outs, Laurence made fewer drawings for publication, preferring to draw only caricatures and sketch portraits of friends for his own amusement. His biting wit and, according to close friends, his "ebullient sense of humour" were readily apparent in these later works. He had an eye for the ridiculous, the incongruous, and the comical side of life, which he transferred to his drawings and letters to his more intimate associates. It was an endearing trait, "which salted a view of the world at large as something to be shocked and pin-pricked and teased into lively apprehension," according to his *Times* obituary.

As a caricaturist he could be painfully frank, even with himself. He drew a self-portrait in a fit of anger at being categorized by Gleeson White as a artist torn between Rossetti and Morris on the one hand, and Ricketts and Houghton on the other. The drawing shows poor Laurence being pulled apart by these formidable figures; a stern mockery of all attempts to restrict and label his individual drawing style. He also drew brief sketches of personalities like H.G. Wells playing tennis, or later of favourite actors and actresses in his plays. His friendship with the period's

"My Landlord at Pembroke Cottage, W.(from life)"
Original pen and ink drawing, Street Library.

Housman's self-portrait "under the divided influence of Rossetti and Morris on the one hand, and Ricketts and A.B.Houghton on the other".
Original pen and ink drawing,
Street Library.

Housman's "H.G.Wells. Attitude while playing tennis?"
Original pen and ink drawing,
Street Library.

supreme caricaturist, Max Beerbohm, was turned into a delightful gesture of self-mockery. One day Max knocked at Laurence's door and asked for a sitting from the newly discovered author of the *Englishwoman's Love-Letters.* Max had been commissioned by *The Tatler,* probably shortly after Laurence was exposed as the true author, and Laurence agreed to the proposal, but only if he was allowed to draw Max as well. As a result, he made at least four versions of his friend as a fine knife-like figure in black ink; while Max drew Laurence as "The Englishwoman?" with a cigarette in his hand (itself an inaccuracy since Laurence never smoked). But there was a mutual respect between the two men, and Laurence owned a small collection of Beerbohm drawings. Although he admired their technical skill, he found even these lost their humour over the years. "I find that to live constantly with the same joke causes it to evaporate," he told Robert Ross, to whom he offered one drawing for £5.[9]

With his new-found wealth, Laurence spent more time exploring the variety of new avenues open to him as a writer.

Max Beerbohm's caricature of Housman,
"The Englishwoman?"
Street Library.

His stage-struck boyhood inspired the decision to pour most of his money into producing his first play. It was called *Bethlehem, A Nativity Play*, and was the first of a long line of dramatic works banned by the overzealous censor of the time – here because it offended the restriction against depicting members of the holy family on stage. But Laurence persisted with his plans, and hired Edward Gordon Craig to design and produce this play privately in 1902. He lost most of his money on that ill-fated production, which had thrown him "in the thick of personal problems", not the least a clash of personalities with his designer.[10] "His beautiful stage-work lent itself to caricature, over which I wickedly engaged myself," Laurence gleefully confessed to Robert

Housman's caricature of Max Beerbohm
Original pen and ink, Street Library.

Ross.[11] But in the end the experience merely strengthened his resolve to succeed in this new and perilous theatrical world.

He was greatly flattered when the theatrical producer Harley Granville-Barker appealed to him to collaborate on a new play, and Laurence wrote his first stage success under his direction. It was called *Prunella, or Love in a Dutch Garden*, a pierrot play which was produced in 1904. Later Laurence published the text in 1906, with a frontispiece drawing of the play's main characters, a pierrot, a foppish rotund dandy, and a beautiful young woman imprisoned behind a locked garden gate. It was a clear homage to Beardsley's pierrot-style drawings, but more detailed and individual in the true Housman style. Then followed his most successful and popular series of plays, *Little Plays of St Francis*, 1922, based on the life of St Francis of Assisi, the text again published with small drawings intended as stage directions for enthusiastic amateur dramatic societies to follow.

Fiction appealed to him as well, and shortly after the triumph of *The English-woman's Love-Letters*, his publishers rushed out his strongly autobiographical novel, *A Modern Antaeus*. He was fascinated by the intimate lives of the members of the royal family and prominent public political figures; and he turned this passion into what many regarded as scandalous satires on the life of Queen Victoria in *Angels and Ministers*, 1921; of George, Duke of Cambridge in *The Life of H.R.H. the Duke of Flamborough,* 1928; and the political wizard Lloyd George in *Timble-rigg*, 1924. Such works inspired plays on the royals as well, like *Pains and Penalties,* which was about the life of Queen Caroline and banned by the censor for the single offending word "adultery". His intimate view of Victoria's life at court in *Victoria Regina* was also banned, until Edward VII intervened and the play was produced to enthusiastic audiences in the summer of the coronation year of 1937. By then Laurence had earned the dubious distinction as "the most censored playwright in England". But the success of this one play marked a turning point in his fortunes, and

he earned £15,000 from the one work alone.

Behind his satires of the royals and politicians lay his sister's outspoken feminist views against a male-dominated government. Laurence learnt to question and doubt the events of the day from Clemence; especially those social injustices which jarred his own conscience. This led to his spending large sums of money to help deserving young people receive university degrees; later he helped to finance the educations of war-torn refugee families. By the turn of the century, most of Clemence's spare moments were spent campaigning for women's suffrage. She introduced Laurence to the extremist Women's Social and Political Union; and he, in turn, lectured and joined the fight, only later backing away when the group's militancy proved too disturbing. But Clemence persisted and fought hard for her beliefs. She made banners and marched for the cause and was outraged by the tax laws which declared a woman must pay taxes, but could not vote. She stocked a rented cottage with borrowed furniture so that the bailiffs would have nothing to seize of her own when they came to collect the money she owed in taxes. As a result she went to Holloway prison on 30 September 1911, and was photographed outside the prison walls, with Laurence beside her for support. When Alfred saw the picture published in the *Evening Standard*, he called it "a lovely portrait of my disreputable relatives", but he was clearly upset by their behaviour. Finally, when the House of Lords took up the issue of women's suffrage, Laurence recalled the ecstatic joy this long-awaited news brought them: "Clem and I fell into each other's arms on the stairs this morning".[12]

Strong-willed, critical yet caring and sympathetic, Clemence remained the most influential person in Laurence's later years. He admired her energy, which allowed her to paint banners and march for women's rights on the one hand, and to spend hours of tedious patient work, engraving the intricate details of his or Guthrie's drawings. She was also an excellent cook and housekeeper, who attended to his domestic needs as she had always done since they arrived together in London. He watched in amazement as she devised new schemes to occupy herself; "exercising those mental muscles of hers which are so like a ramping and roaring lion if given no outlet".[13] She was the character of Marcia, the strong, able woman he created in *A Modern Antaeus*: "I'm too strong for my sex...There are so many things I *can* do, and mayn't. It never strikes a man, I suppose, what a prison this is? You don't want to thread needles, and darn stockings, or wear your hair long; all things you could do if you wished. If you want to break out, you break out, and that's the difference, But look at me!"

Laurence always believed he would not live to an old age, but would die at sixty-seven, "his lucky number". To mark the event, the preceeding year he wrote his own obituary and sent it to his old employer, the *Manchester Guardian*. They paid him for it, but it was not published until twenty-seven years later. He called it "Without Regret". It remains a terse account, written "in a spirit of mild mockery", of his life primarily as a writer, activist and playwright; he surprisingly failed even to mention his artistic career. At the root of this obituary was a deep-seated fear of posterity. He had long shared Alfred's fear of an invasion of his privacy, and he now wanted to leave an ordered account of his varied activities and opinions, unhampered by the speculation or error he feared after his death. As early as 1905 he had written to Robert Ross, "By the way, I forbid you to publish my private letters after my death! It is quite necessary to say that to *you*. I have carefully elaborated my posthumous character; & a very few extracts from my real epistles would explode it."[14] To another friend, who had written in search of Housman's photograph and autograph, Laurence wrote back with obvious delight, "my portrait can't be got either from me or from the photographers. While I'm alive I value my privacy — I've no use for it when I'm dead — let him wait till then."[15]

Laurence and Clemence left London during wartime, and took a cottage on the edge of the New Forest. In 1923 they moved to be near friends at the delightful village of Street in Somerset. There they built their own house, Long Meadow, in their friend's orchard, and lived together peacefully in a country routine which echoed their own childhoods. Laurence would write in his study at the far end of the garden, or prepare his plans for the local dramatic society productions, for which Clemence helped to sew the costumes. In 1937 he completed his surprisingly frank autobiography, *The Unexpected Years* – the title an indication he had not expected to enjoy such a variety of experiences in later life.

When Clemence died in December 1955, Laurence remained at Long Meadow. The villagers remembered him as "a familiar figure who still continued his interest in local dramatics", having acted in as well as directed their productions. He was a much loved figure; "bearded, black-hatted and shopping bag in hand, he was frequently seen on early morning shopping expeditions".[16] Four years later he died, on 20 February 1959, at nearby Glastonbury, where he had directed the drama festival between the wars. He left behind a legacy of some eighty books which spanned a working and creative life of over fifty years. Unfortunately this fact was somewhat overshadowed by his outspoken later years as a pacifist; "the uneasy cuckoo in the nest" according to his *Times* obituary. But it was a deserved tribute to a versatile and active campaigner for peace and humanity in the world: "The belligerent suffragist, the pugnacious pacifist, the intellectual nihilist, the dubious Socialist, the lover of cats, the romantic moralist, the English anti-rationalist, the all but Christian critic of institutional Christianity – all were of a peace; whether as idealist or iconoclast, it was hard for him to be moderate."[17]

Jump to Glory Jane, *1892*.

Laurence Housman and The Critics

aurence Housman was taught to seek out critical opinions of his work at an early period in his career. But it was not until he produced drawings and book designs which were reviewed at length in the influential papers and magazines of his day and become a critic himself, that he experienced a greater tolerance and respect for the critic's role. He was fascinated by the power of words in the articles, reviews, poems, stories and plays he wrote; but unlike his fellow authors and journalists he maintained a lifelong respect for the influence critics could exert over their subjects. He was aware that in a few select phrases they had the power to establish an artist's reputation, or condemn a career into obscurity. And he was deeply concerned by this power; especially when it was wielded over his fellow artists' reputations. Unfortunately his increased fervour and skill with words also led to misunderstandings and controversy, especially during his final years as a Guardian art critic. For example, he outraged his fellow critic, Roger Fry, by attacking an exhibition of William Rothenstein's paintings in 1910. Fry wrote to console the artist and his distraught wife: "It means that there is much more in them than can be appreciated at once. You have to suffer this but it's really the greatest possible compliment. I don't know Housman enough to know whether there is concealed malice in this or only incapacity to see."[1]

He was also fascinated by the struggle for artistic fame and reputation; it was one of the reasons he remained devoted to Oscar Wilde even after his fall. But then he lived in an age of "instant fame"; when artists and writers could be rocketted to notice almost overnight, especially if they had discovered some new style or means to shock or challenge established conventions of taste. Aubrey Beardsley died a master of this technique. Even after his untimely death in 1898 his reputation continued to inspire: "How really inimitable his manner was is already proven," wrote Gleeson White in his famous *Studio* obituary of Beardsley. "The short five years that he was before the public sufficed for the growth and withering of imitators. None could raise the flower though all had got the seed...Death has given Aubrey Beardsley mortality of youth; and in future histories of illustration, whether for blame or praise, men must add that it was a mere boy who did these things, and did them as no other attempted them before."[2]

But as Laurence discovered to his dismay, there was often a wide gap between artistic reputation and financial reward, at least in his chosen field of illustration. For this reason, he fluctuated between drawing, designing books, writing stories, articles and reviews, never certain of his income from any one field. "My indifference to a paying popularity has, I believe, in the long run helped and not hindered my output of the things which seemed to me most worth doing," he admitted in one of the characteristically frank passages of his autobiography. He only regretted the "large disproportion between the respectable reputation which I began to acquire in my early thirties, and the monetary return I got from it".[3]

Oscar Wilde taught him an artist's duty was to himself as well as his public; but in the end an artist could not turn his back on that public. Laurence responded with: "whether one wills it or no, one has to belong". It was a lesson he used to preface his autobiography, his own account of a long and successful career: "I have given more conformity than allegiance to the powers that be; and the conventions which impose themselves. But however little it conforms or tenders allegiance, no life worth living can be isolated from the lives of others."[4]

His literary success was nurtured by this lesson as well. Laurence knew too well the power of critics' judgements by the time he had prepared *An Englishwoman's Love-Letters*. In a sense the book was his successful triumph over the critics; a calculated attempt to manipulate their power for his own ends. For example, he defiantly remained the anonymous author, despite considerable pressure from critics determined to unmask the identity of this overnight literary sensation. Surely his love of practical jokes and understanding of the way the critic passed his judgements allowed him to thoroughly enjoy the outrageous suggestions made by some of the period's most influential critics. Some believed his book was written by Queen Victoria, or Alice Meynell or Marie Corelli; American critics were convinced it was the work of Edith Wharton or Elizabeth von Arnim. Most were sure the author was a woman. *The Academy* praised its sympathetic feminine style; that of an "exquisite nature...lit by the fine pure flame of her soul". George Meredith recommended it to a woman friend and declared it "worth reading as a cry from the heart. Should the letters prove to be fictitious, we have a genius in literature."[5]

Three months after publication, with sales booming and numerous pirated editions published in America, Laurence still refused to reveal his authorship. He believed the longer he kept his secret, the more prolonged the chance of greater book sales, and his agent agreed. As late as March 1901, he refused to admit that he was indeed the author, then despite the fact that *The Academy* had unmasked him a month earlier. At this point he learnt a valuable and lasting lesson about critical fame and artistic success. For those critics who once praised the book now turned viciously against it and its author. They attacked the work for "its narrow and unhealthy tone". His fictional account of a young woman's love for a young man – who eventually thwarts her and condemns her to die of a broken heart – was now too calculated. Critics deplored the "unworthy nature of the confession", called it a deception which at most was "boring" and "in no way remarkable" (*Sunday Chronicle*). When Laurence sent his brother Alfred a copy, he found it embarassing, and sent it on to their younger brother Herbert, who read and enjoyed it as he prepared to fight in the Boer War. In America, where at least seven pirated editions had appeared before an authorized edition was published, *The Bookman* editor published Edith Wharton's hilarious parody letters ("Ownest — I was just dangling one timorous creamy magnolia-white foot over the edge of the bed, into the icy crackling void of circumambient cold..."). Previously, the same editor had published a three page review of the book.

And yet for all the outrage of critics, and readers who felt duped by his hoax, Laurence triumphed in the end. His book entered an eighth edition and earned him a small fortune which transformed his domestic life. And although he later dismissed it as the "worst" of his books, he was clearly pleased with this triumph over his critics and the public alike.[6]

* * * * * * * * * * * *

Laurence Housman's career as a book designer and illustrator received a generally mixed reception by the critics. His influential Lane designs were largely ignored by reviewers who either concentrated upon the literary content of the books or lumped his designs with the Lane school of artists. The conservative barometer of Victorian literary taste, *The Athenaeum,* was surprisingly one of Laurence's earliest champions, especially of his stories and poems. But the progressive arts and crafts oriented *The Studio* magazine, under the editorship of Gleeson White, was his greatest champion. Here appeared the most substantial and perceptive reviews published either full or half-page, with Housman's illustrations or binding designs reproduced.

Laurence was largely philosophical about the stinging attacks and lavish praise of his critics; on the whole, "these divided opinions did not much trouble me". In fact he was most pleased by literary reviews, like the enthusiastic remarks he received for his fairy-tales from Dr Richard Garnett, then reviewer of *The Sketch* as

well as Keeper of Printed Books at the British Museum. Garnett "had given my fairy-tales a welcome with higher praises than I should have given them myself," Laurence recalled with obvious pleasure. He added, "though the illustrations were liked by few, the stories were generally commended, and have had sufficient life in them to recover from the 'out-of-print' condition into which they lapsed a few years after publication".

Just how sales of his books were affected by the illustrations is suggested by the fact they were especially unpopular with the conservative provincial booksellers. Laurence learnt this from Kegan Paul, who had been told by his touring salesman that strong objections had been raised by booksellers to the Housman style of illustration. In fact the salesman himself disliked them,

Housman's grotesque fantasies were often attacked by the critics and public:
a) "The Man Who Killed the Cuckoo"

b) "The Shadow-Weavers", both from A Farm in Fairyland, *1894.*

Housman's figures were attacked for distortions and poor anatomical drawing: "Homestead Westward in the Blue Mountains", to Weird Tales, *1893.*

---

for he "not merely failed to find a market for them, but was met with derision when he offered them". He claimed they "hurt his sense of dignity; and also his standing with the trade". Laurence pondered the situation and concluded "the right solution was for him to agree heartily with my detractors, but to say that just now they were 'the thing', and that his firm had to publish them to meet a depraved taste". Such was his ability to turn a disappointment into a comical joke. In this case it was a trick he borrowed from a friend who had overheard two children discussing his illustrations, the one scolding the other for failing to appreciate the drawings: "She must like them – they were 'the thing'."[7]

Tailpiece from Goblin Market, *1893.*

THE BOOKS AND THEIR CRITICS

Jump to Glory Jane, 1892

Laurence's first serious attempt at illustration received a mixed reception by the critics. It was published in the autumn of 1892, and *The Times* (27 October 1892) was less than enthusiastic: "The literary budget of the past week is considerably more remarkable for quantity than quality, and from this reproach it is not saved by the publication, in book-form, of some curious verses by Mr George.Meredith, entitled Jump to Glory Jane." However despite the "rather far-fetched" poem and dismissive remarks about Quilter's introduction, Laurence's illustrations were praised for their success in such uninspired company: "Mr Housman, the artist, has discharged his difficult task well. His outlines are quaint without being 'burlesque', and they reflect something of the essential sadness of the episode."

Later, when the critics had a chance to compare the work with other Housman designs, they agreed while it was technically weak, it suggested hints of stronger work to follow. *The Artist* review of his career up to 1898, declared this first book was worth greater attention: "Blundering in technique as it is, and at times almost ludicrous in drawing, he has never done anything more vigorously expressive; his critics, even when unfavourable, all allowed that his work was almost marvellously in key with the poem." Gleeson White went further. Writing in the *Magazine of Art* in 1899, he thought Laurence's drawings showed "evidence of personal expression, even if immature. The bizarre legend is depicted grotesquely, as it should be, but also seriously; you do not laugh at the jumping saint, even if a smile of tolerance is forced from you." He noted how Laurence had created a "sympathetic view of the religious-obsessed Jane", which made the viewer "feel a certain respect for its eccentric effort towards perfection". He noted the influence of Houghton's *Graphic* drawings of Shakers in America, but believed a greater sympathy was evident in Housman's work. "It is just because Mr Housman, despite its paradox and satire,reveals a curiously insistent tolerance, combined with insistent hatred of all selfishness and pain that you are tempted to reckon him among the preachers."

By the turn of the century, Laurence had ended his drawing career, and critics had a better chance to assess the drawings. Then their opinions were more enthusiastic. R.E.D. Sketchley in his pioneering *English Book Illustration of Today,* 1903, was convinced Laurence had "hardly ever surpassed these designs". The literary critic Charles Kains-Jackson wrote in *The Book-Lover's Magazine* in 1908 how the drawings "excite a curious interest with a combined strong sense of the mystic". The strong art nouveau linearity of the figures attracted John Russell Taylor in his pioneering *The Art Nouveau Book in Britain,* 1966. He believed they were distinctive distillations of Rossetti and Houghton, "but at the same time with an arching intensity and mannerist exaggeration which were unmistakably Ninetyish". It was a unique achievement which "at once attracted attention", not the least for its "novelty of style, and the expressiveness of the way the pictures were related to the hand-written text".

On the other hand, as historians studied further the vast output of Nineties illustrated literature, critical judgements, of this first book in particular, became more objective. Percy Muir, for example, in his more wide-ranging survey, *Victorian Illustrated Books,* 1971, dismissed the entire venture by first quoting Sketchley's praise, then adding "no more unfortunate judgement could be passed on the unfortunate artist. For this was a disastrous piece of book-making and failure is by no means entirely to be laid at the artist's door....The author called it a satire. It is in fact a joke that does not come off. The mixture of spindly letterpress and calligraphy in the text is extremely unfortunate, and Housman had not yet acquired the ability that he showed a couple of years later in his successful marriage of text and drawing in Jane Barlow's *The End of Elfin-Town.*"

Goblin Market, 1893

When Laurence's illustrated edition of Christina Rossetti's poem appeared late in 1893, it marked a change in attitude by his critics, and he was taken more seriously as an artist. The prestigious *Athenaeum* review included the book in its Christmas list (23 December 1893), alongside reviews of poetry and illustration which included his beloved Arthur Hughes's edition of *Sing-Song, a Nursery Rhyme Book* ("beautiful in feeling and beautifully drawn"). It was a serious review, which announced "a new edition of Miss Rossetti's well-known poem, illustrated with artistic designs, at once masculine and vigorous, by Mr L. Housman, some of which are better than others, although all have merit. The best, we think, the goblins in the orchard, Laura on the bank of the pool, and the goblins belabouring Laura."

The Studio had reproduced the binding in its Arts and Crafts exhibition review, but Gleeson White decided to give the book further prominence in his substantial review, illustrated with three drawings from the book, "to show what a delightful little volume it is". Here he also attempted the first serious and critical assessment of Laurence's style: "Mr Housman is rapidly discovering the hardest problem to an artist — himself. Although redolent of the Millais of the Once-a-Week school, no less than the strongly individual work of Mr Charles Ricketts, there is sign of a distinctly personal note which promises much. One might exhaust many good superlatives in praise of this daintiest of dainty books. Caviare to the many, to the few who enjoy fancy and finely imagined ornament it offers

more decorative suggestions in its small compass than any volume of equal size can recall." And he continued to praise the book until his death in 1898; writing in the posthumously published article for the *Magazine of Art* in 1899, that *Goblin Market* was "perhaps the most charming bound volume, with the single exception of *Silverpoints* [designed by Ricketts] that has yet been issued by any publisher".

Turn of the century critics agreed that the book was one of Housman's most successful. *The Book-Lover's Magazine* in 1908 claimed the drawings were an early example "of capturing the improbable in the net of probability". They were "verifications of the poetess's hypotheses — for they amount to that — are splendid. They realise the life of the small animals *à merveille.*" They predicted it would become "a treasure" for collectors; which indeed it was when published in standard, large paper and even miniature editions. By the 1920s the drawings were linked with their predecessor: Forrest Reid in his survey *Illustrators of the Eighteen Sixties,* 1928. called it "a worthy successor" to Rossetti's early version of his sister's poem. "This delightful little book shows how admirably Mr Housman carries on the Pre-Raphaelite tradition, without sacrificing his own individuality." And although Percy Muir doubted the wisdom of Reid's judgement ("It is indeed a very pretty book but the praise is too high."), more recent scholars agreed with Reid. When the drawings were exhibited at a fantasy illustration exhibition in America, the catalogue acknowledged "while owing a debt to Rossetti's illustrations, Housman's compositions have none of their dreamlike quality and are far more horrific in nature ....Nevertheless, when *Goblin Market* is mentioned, Housman's intense images usually come to mind rather than Rossetti's."[8]

The End of Elfin-Town, 1894

The rich vein of fantasy Laurence had successfully begun to mine in *Goblin Market* continued to attract the admirers of his next book. Macmillan also published this fantasy volume, which appeared late in 1894, again in time for Christmas sales. *The Athenaeum* grouped it with other Christmas offerings in its review (22 December 1894), and claimed it contained not only "spirited verses, fresh and full of vivacity, and with picturesque phrases that are in keeping with the narrative, which is quaint and attractive in itself"; but the designs also "suit the poem they illustrate, for they are original, picturesque, varied, and full of passion". The distorted and elongated figures which many critics later objected to appealed to the *Athenaeum's* critic: "Unlike the majority of draughtsmen with pen and pencil, he knows how to draw the human figure with taste and precision; his sole shortcoming in this respect is the slightness and gauntness of his representations of the youth of Fairyland. Apart from this, nothing can be prettier than the Fays delineated on pp.48 and 51."

The most substantial review again came from *The Studio*, where Gleeson White devoted a full page (with one illustration) on his "The Editor's Room" page. In it he gave the first assessment of the Housman influence on current illustration and book design. He began on an unpromising note; that the story of Elfin-Town was "hardly worth a more serious treatment than the trivial jingle in which it is told". But in Laurence's hands his "exquisite designs" gave the story new life. "Mr Housman has obviously studied D.G.Rossetti through the medium of Messrs Ricketts and Shannon. Yet, as he excells Rossetti in vigour of drawing and composition, as witness the amazing tangle of limbs in the first of the full-page illustrations, so has he fortunately escaped the mannerism, the spindle-like attenuation of legs and arms, which disfigures the more recent productions of The Vale—e.g. the *Hero and Leander* and *Sphinx.*" He rightly declared Laurence's title-page of five winged archers standing over a dead prince an homage to Beardsley: "Still, Mr Housman displays a conspicuous sense of physical beauty that Mr Beardsley has lost, or, if he retains it, has this long past been studiously suppressing. Of so rare and delicate a

grace are the winged forms which occur at the heading and those of the several sections that one cannot but regret that the artist has chosen to fashion them merely as half-length statues, ending in terminal pillars, instead of completing them to their full and perfect proportions. A long search would fail to discover a more refined and faultless beauty of face and hands than those of the figure at the beginning of Part III, The Flitting."

Gleeson White was himself a talented book designer, as well as a reviewer, so that when he declared Housman's work a major new influence upon the art of the illustrated book, it was very high praise indeed. His review ended in light of this new pronouncement, by suggesting how best Laurence might master those occasional lapses into sloppiness which damaged the unity of his designs. "While, however, taken by itself, each and every one of Mr Housman's drawings, as such, is admirable, it must be confessed that they fall short when judged from the point of view of decoration; that, like Rossetti's illustrations to Tennyson and Christina Rossetti, they are not integral parts of the volume in which they appear. The cover of the book has a conventional diaper of dainty, if somewhat thin, design, which would lead one to expect some sort of attempt at decoration of the page within. As a matter of fact, there is none. If only Mr Housman could be persuaded to devote more attention to the quality of his work as decoration in black and white, to be sparing of shading, to be less laboured in treatment, and in general to adopt a bolder scheme of massing the lighter in contrast to the darker portions of his compositions, with his very extraordinary gifts of draughtsmanship and originality of imagination, he might easily attain to be second to none among the book-decorators of the century." Later, in his *Magazine of Art* article in 1899, he was more specific, and attacked his fellow critics for criticizing the drawings as "morbid"; this was only a term used "by the puzzled". Housman had used the more "passion-frought" elements of life and "incorporated the uncanny, unholy mystery" in his vision of fairyland where "the figures are strangely unlike those of Sir Noel Paton or the old-time Christmas card". In the end this made the book more "thrilling" than its sentimental predecessors; the work of a youthful, novel artist of greater confidence.

The Elfin-Town drawings established Laurence as a fairy illustrator in the eyes of future generations of critics. *The Book-Lover's Magazine* in 1908 was convinced, "the artist is already coming into his kingdom in which we shall soon come to know him as unquestioned master even as we know a Burne-Jones, a Fred Walker, a Linley Sambourne, or Sime. There is always something of greatness about this separateness. It is said in the word Distinction." Even the more cautious Percy Muir agreed with such praise; he found the Elfin-Town drawings "a successful marriage of text and drawing" which, with the Goblin Market drawings, were "incomparably the most successful examples of his work as an illustrator".

A Farm in Fairyland, 1894

This first collection of illustrated fairy-tales appeared the same time as *The End of Elfin-Town,* and some critics reviewed the two books together. For example, Gleeson White wrote of Elfin-Town in *The Studio:* "The public which, but a month or two since, was struck with admiration of Mr Laurence Housman's *A Farm in Fairyland,* in which he surpassed himself, were scarcely prepared for him to follow it up so quickly, and that too with a work of even higher merit than the last." In fact reviews of this collection of stories were the most substantial to date. It was noticed not only by *The Athenaeum* and *The Studio,* but also by the *Pall Mall Gazette, The Times, Daily News, Manchester Guardian, The Speaker* as well as the influential illustrated papers *The Sketch* and *The Graphic.* In America it was reviewed by *The Critic,* the influential New York literary magazine which largely dismissed the book.

The reviews generally emphasized the literary qualities of the stories, which marked Laurence out as a talented fantasy writer. The most enthusiastic and gratifying to Laurence was written by Dr Garnett in *The Sketch,* who explained there had been a recent flood of fairy-tale books of which many "have merited the epithets of graceful and charming. 'A Farm in Fairyland', by Laurence Housman, is, nevertheless, divided from the best of them, so far as is known to us, by a gulf which we cannot denote better than by describing the author's place as on the right side of the boundary of genius. While positively thrilling by the originality of his conceptions, he charms by their simplicity." He praised the intricate, yet clear plots, filled with "weird fancy" and "mystic glamour"; they offered surprises and delights because they forced the unsuspecting reader to ask "the half-angry question, 'Why did I not think of this myself?'" In language "most fully appreciated by adults" but clearly not "beyond the range of children, whom his fancy and humour will especially delight", Laurence had written and illustrated a collection of remarkable stories. "Those acquainted with Mr Housman's previous achievements as an artist will not need to be told that his illustrations to his own book are full of imagination," Garnett added at the end of his review.

The Athenaeum offered a more restrained, yet equally encouraging review: "We have seldom read stories which have afforded us more pleasure than the first five of this book. They are written with strong poetical feeling, and show much lively fancy – or we might say imagination – and a warm love of birds, beasts, and flowers. Besides this they are original. We do not like the rest of the stories so much, but the five good ones are possessions in themselves." The critic of *The Speaker* also admired his imagination: "The illustrations are distinguished by much originality and inventiveness in design. Sometimes the effect is very charming, as in the title-page and frontispiece, but sometimes Mr Housman's originality expresses itself in eccentricity rather than beauty." Praise also came from the *Manchester Guardian* critic, (whom Laurence was shortly to replace), who singled out the drawings as "weird, imaginative, and full of talent".

On the other hand, the book's adverse critics objected to its grotesque themes and exaggerated drawings. The *Pall Mall Gazette* found it "confused, and not very attractive"; but this was tempered by their belief that "we have no doubt that any child who gets these stories for a Christmas present will derive a good deal of enjoyment from them". *The Graphic*, still a source of some of the period's most striking illustrations, declared it "full of dainty conceits, provided young readers are not frightened away by the eccentric illustrations".

The most critical attacks came from the large circulation daily newspapers – which could not have helped book sales. *The Times* dismissed it because it "does not specially tempt us, and the fantastic engravings are somewhat grim". *The Guardian* critic failed to understand the title, and found the "very unequal stories" too much a mixture of the "charming" and the "disagreeable"; although "on the whole, the collection is above the average of modern fairy stories". Similarly, the *Daily News* attacked it for pretentiousness and obscure symbolism: "The first thing that strikes one is the gaunt figure of a medieaval ploughman, apparently about sixteen feet high, upon the sage-green cover. This is merely one of the passing eccentricities of the hour. The book itself is not all of a revolutionary character, presenting as it does merely some mild little fairy tales told in studiously simple language."

Gleeson White wrote the most intelligent and revealing review in *The Studio*. He began with praise: "There are some books – singularly few – which as they fall into a critic's hands, so delight him that his appreciation is in danger of becoming a mere rhapsody. This is one; and the present writer, wearied of reading the new books of the season, sick of most of their pictures and pattern, was deploring the lack of invention or power they evinced, when he lighted upon it, and straightaway forgot everything else as he read it cover to cover." Having reviewed Housman's previous books, "the delightful drawings here were not unexpected, although far beyond any previous attempts. As an author he

meets him here for the second time only; but yet the book has at once become one of the few that he would not readily forget." He goes on to discuss Housman's influences; that Ricketts was his "single model", which was a dangerous path to follow. He urged him to turn his back on such an obvious model, "not merely to escape disaster, but to work out his own way in a manner that must please the master as much as it does credit to the disciple". The direction he should take was suggested in the steady, even line he had obviously borrowed from the "Once-a-Week school" of engraved illustration: "It is evident in every line he sets down, and withal he is himself full of invention, full of power." He concluded with a recommendation: "If you care for delicious fantasies in prose, or in picture, get this little book." Later he was more cautious about certain aspects of the drawings. Writing in the *Magazine of Art* in 1899, he then had the chance to compare it with Housman's subsequent story collections, and concluded: "The initial letters are his own, and extremely charming, but beyond pleasantly proportioned margins and excellently placed typography, the style of each does not differ noticeably from the work of any good publisher."

But the most damning review came from America, where the book was published by Dodd Mead & Co. and reviewed by the powerful *The Critic* magazine (15 December 1894). Here he was accused of affectation and insincerity, his elongated creatures, stumpy gnomes and picturesque landscapes apparently too rarefied a vision for American readers: "Just what connection a good and simple technique can have with an affectation of the grotesque on the side of invention, we do not know, but Mr Lawrence (sic) Housman combines the two in a remarkable degree." The drawings were more objectionable and "queerer" than the fairy-tales: "There are towers as big as a band-box, and drapery with shell-like folds, and tree-trunks like hempen ropes, and figures like disjointed marionettes. We dislike to see talent so wasted; but others may like it."

The House of Joy, 1895

This second collection of illustrated fairy-tales appeared in December 1895, and was successful enough to merit a second edition that same year. The stories were again praised more than the illustrations. *The Saturday Review* claimed they marked the debut of a children's fantasy writer to rival Oscar Wilde or even Hans Andersen: "Since the publication of [Oscar Wilde's] 'The House of Pomegranates' nothing so worthy has been done in the domain of modern fairy-tale as Mr Laurence Housman's 'House of Joy'." The eight tales were "distinguished by that archaic sentiment and that wonderful beauty of line which are already associated with the name of Laurence Housman". Some, like "The Story of the Herons" and "The White King" were "as good as Andersen at his best, coloured with a curiously modern tinge". But unlike Andersen, they were marred by obsessive gloom, which was their one major fault: "Even in the most melancholy of Andersen's tales the lightness of his heart shines through, but one never feels that Laurence Housman's heart is light. His style, fastidious and graceful though it is, lacks the magic of the Scandinavian, the silver tone which even a translation has failed to obscure. This is, of course, to compare Mr Laurence Housman with the greatest master of his art, and the 'House of Joy' justifies use of the comparison."

The critic of *The New Age* agreed with the *Saturday Review*, and found the stories secured Laurence an "honourable place" among the numerous volumes in what amounted to a revival of illustrated fairy tales. But his collection stood apart from his rivals, as "a marked and striking improvement both in power of imagination and in excellence of style. The stories have originality, fantasy, and beauty; the illustrations are unique."

Praise for the illustrations came from *The Speaker* critic as well: "I have never seen any black-and-white work by Mr Housman which satisfies me so much as the pictures to the 'House of Joy'. The harshness, amounting almost to crudity, of some of his earlier designs has vanished. The eager imaginative quality remains; I instance the designs for 'The Prince with Nine Sorrows', 'The Luck of the Roses', and 'Happy Returns' as reaching the high water-mark of imaginative black-and-white work in our time." *The Guardian* agreed that it was "one of the prettiest of Christmas volumes. Type and paper, illustrations and text, are alike attractive." The newly established journal of fine illustration, *Black and White*, claimed the book was "exquisitely wrought and exquisitely illustrated. The writing and the drawing are alike imbued with imagination and distinction."

Perhaps the most gratifying review came from R.A.M.Stevenson, art critic of the *Manchester Guardian*, whom Laurence had recently replaced, although Stevenson continued to review books there. He declared the stories "among the most original and charming fairy-tales of the season. Mr Housman writes as well as he designs. He is a born story-teller. His fairy romances are not only quite new, but they flow from his pen as naturally as if he were telling them to children... We do not know any living writer whose stories are more certain to please children, although these will give unbounded satisfaction to their elders as well." When he focused on the illustrations, he was generally more cautious; in later reviews pointing out annoying anatomical inaccuracies and eccentricities. But here he was enthusiastic: "The merits of Mr Housman's designs are better known. Though peculiar, they are not eccentric. The flowing lines of Mr Housman's compositions and their richness of tone distinguish them clearly from the work of any other draughtsman, and at the same time make them beautiful in spite of minor faults." Laurence found Stevenson's remarks intelligent and useful; and he would always remember the comment that "the heads of his figures, for instance, are now and then preposterously small".

The Athenaeum reviewed the book as usual, although the review was not published until nearly half a year after publication. This was probably just as well, since for once it was far from complimentary:

"Mr L.Housman writes well, and has a good deal of fancy. Sometimes, indeed, he has almost too much for it carries him and his stories into shadowy regions, whither it is difficult for plain readers and reviewers to follow." The illustrations were dismissed in two smug sentences: "Mr Housman himself seems to be responsible for the illustrations. They are far from being good."

Green Arras, 1896

By the time this first book of poems was published, late in 1896, Laurence Housman had reached the height of his critical reputation as an artist. Walter Crane praised his contributions to black-and-white illustration and linked him with the so-called "Studio School" of Gleeson White. This placed him alongside fellow artists like Patten Wilson, Fairfax Muckley, Charles Robinson. But, according to Crane, only Housman was notable "for remarkable taste in ornament, and a numerous poetic fancy".[9]

Reviewers of *Green Arras* noted how it was yet another instance of his versatility as an artist, story-teller and now poet. The most significant review came from *The Athenaeum*, where two full pages were devoted to it in Housman's new role as a poet. The magazine could be quite personal with its critical remarks, aimed at those artists and literary figures it felt substantial enough to review. It was as if they felt in some way responsible for their reputations, and tried to make sure they did not go too far astray from the limitations set out in early reviews of their works. *Green Arras* then, was greeted as yet another production by a protégé: "The circle of Mr Housman's admirers widens slowly and steadily. And to them he owes a duty – for they expect much of him, and cry their expectations from the very housetops. Much, however, as they expect and follow his erratic evolutions, to acquiesce in his startling conclusions, and, hardest of all, to assent to his somewhat capricious estimate of the value of words...Mr Housman would seem to desire recognition in the character of a great master of words." Comparisons were made between Rossetti's poems, and the nonesense inventions of Lewis Carroll, especially Alice's dialogue with Humpty Dumpty. The reviewer was especially "sympathetic" to these dream-world inventions: "Mr Housman has produced passages – sometimes whole poems – full of music subtle and rich, full of thought, always fine, and now and then deep and high." Housman's versatility was stressed, especially his strong visual sense: "But one must remember – being forced to the remembrance by sterling qualities and strong defects – that here is work from a hand trained to express itself in two mediums, and borrowing qualities from the one for the other. Every poem or passage in which the author succeeds has the power of making us see a picture." In the end the book was unique; it "sometimes evades analysis – a book of strange virtues and defects. It reflects, we hope with the same promise of ultimate performance, the qualities which in his other art have won recognition for its author... Outwardly and visibly the book is triumphant in its own type of beauty." And while the illustrations were "as unequal as the verse", the book "with all its faults and shortcomings, is the work of a poet".

Gleeson White reproduced the frontispiece in his *Studio* review, hoping it "will afford the reader an idea of its remarkable characteristics". He too stressed it was the work of a remarkable versatility, written, designed and illustrated "by the same hand. The uniformity of result is as pleasant as it is uncommon." His interest in fine bindings and cover designs made him conclude the book "deserves the attention of the bibliophile". His enthusiasm continued when he published his review of Housman's illustrations in the *Magazine of Art* in 1899. Then the book's title borders were "still more marvelously wrought" than even Housman's two previous fairy-tale collections: "To say that these title-pages stand absolutely alone, and that no other artist, living or dead, has done work like them, is mere fact; to add that no living artist could beat them in the fastidiously delicate embroidery of their penwork, is a statement one may risk with a light heart. Yet they are not without breadth and largeness of design; and if you wish it gained with less effort you have but to turn to the end-papers to find it." It was a unique example of intricate pen draughtsmanship, "treated in a way no pen-draughtsman to-day seems to attempt".

The most serious criticism and "caustic" comment came, as we have seen, from Laurence's brother Alfred, to whom he had sent the book's manuscript and proof illustrations before publication. Alfred's comments on the drawings deserve examination, since they played the largest role in the evolution of *Green Arras* as we know it. A typical remark dismissed his heavily draped figures as "wind-blown pillow-cases". His letter of 26 September 1896 offered similar frank comments on his favourite drawings and Laurence included this letter in his memorial biography of *Alfred, My Brother: A.E. Housman*, 1937, so much had it affected him.

Alfred began the letter on a specific note: "Of the illustrations I like *The Queen's Bees* the best, with its distant view & its kidney bean sticks: the scarecrow is full of life & is perhaps the best of your wind-blown pillow-cases to date; & the figure in the foreground wins upon one when one realises that what one at first took for his nose is really & truly his chin. *The Corn-keeper* looks much better than it did in Atalanta. The central or principal figure in *The Housebuilders* strikes me as very good indeed, if his right arm were a trifle shorter; but if I were the employer of those bricklayers I should take care to pay them by the piece & not by the day."

Such was his concern over the drawings that he included his own sketches, to illustrate the meeting in "The Keepsake", and "White Rabbits": "I am much disappointed to find no illustration to *White Rabbits*. I have attempted to supply this deficiency & I enclose the result. You will see that I have had some difficulty with the young lady's arm; & the gentleman is not quite as tall as I could have wished. The moon (together with the weather-vane &

everything else which I could not draw) is behind the spectator, which accounts for the vivid illumination of the principal figures. You may remark that the rabbits are not running: true; but they have been running, & they are just going to begin again."[9]

All-Fellows, 1896

This collection of seven legends, with religious verses, appeared late in 1896, and was largely overshadowed by *Green Arras*. Critics neglected to review it and only later did Gleeson White attempt to restore its position as a "book of fantasy which those who love regard too deeply to attempt to analyze". It contained "some of his most matured illustrations". Later still Charles Kains-Jackson praised its drawings as "exceedingly beautiful, intense in feeling, lovely in design".

The Field of Clover, 1898

This new collection of illustrated stories appeared in December, 1898. It marked a new spate of critical attention and on the whole was a commercial success. It went into a second edition, was published in America, and was produced in a large paper edition for collectors (see appendix).

The Athenaeum reviewer seemed puzzled by this new "story-book", whose title "may or may not have some connexion with its contents. It is possibly intended to signify to young readers that they will find dainty and delicate food inside the cover. This is the fact, for Mr Housman is full of poetic fancy." Although Gleeson White had died before publication, *The Studio* continued his policy of substantial review space to each new Housman volume. Here they reproduced the frontispiece alongside its review of a book they claimed "an example of the work of the artist at his best". The stories alone "breathe the spirit of the world of fantasy, and are far and away beyond the average stories of their class. The author's illustrations are full of strange interest and artistic distinction."

The most interesting review came for the first time from *The Dome*, a well produced and illustrated fine art magazine then in its second year. Laurence had in fact contributed to its first number (see appendix) so it was not surprising to see his work reviewed here. It was in fact a substantial review, which included a double-page reproduction of the frontispiece and title page. Reviewed with other noted illustrated editions, including E.J.Sullivan's edition of Carlyle's *Sartor Resartus*, Laurence's book was reserved for the final paragraphs. It was, however, largely a dismissive review. The critic praised his drawings on their own, but not as successful book illustrations: "As a performance on literature, *The Field of Clover* does not strike us as being equal to some other collections of tales by Mr Housman... But it is not inconsistent with this to say that it is nevertheless far better than most books of its kind; while the illustrations, with which in this notice we are mainly concerned, would make it worth having even if the literary content were further below the general average than they are below Mr Housman's own."

The Sensitive Plant, 1898

When Housman's drawings to Shelley's poem appeared late in 1898, it was largely ignored by the critics. Only later was the book given its proper place. According to Charles Kains-Jackson in *The Book-Lover's Magazine*, 1908, the illustrations were "beyond what any of the great illustrators of the Victorian era from 1850 -70 achieved. It has the precision and the decision, the design and the detail of the great pre-Raphaelities, but it is free from their invincible quaintness."

The Little Land, 1899

Kains-Jackson continued his praises with this "remarkable and little-known volume", which appeared in mid 1899. First published by Grant Richards, it was later reissued by Elkin Mathews. The four illustrations engraved by Clemence were examples of "the author at his highest in purely imaginative work". Not every critic agreed, however. When *The Athenaeum* reviewed it (26 August, 1899), they failed to mention the drawings and concentrated on attacking its literary weakness. It was one of the most disappointing reviews Laurence received, and marked a low in his critical reputation. "We read Mr Laurence Housman's successive volumes of verse – the last is The Little Load (sic) (Grant Richards) – with growing dissatisfaction. His work seems to proceed entirely from the will and intention to write, not the necessity." In the end the book failed to reach "beyond mediocrity".

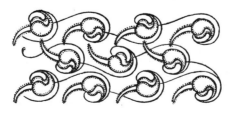

Tailpiece from Goblin Market, *1893.*

THE CRITICAL REPUTATION

By the turn of the century, just when Housman was about to abandon illustration for writing, a number of perceptive surveys and critical articles of his work appeared. None hinted that he had turned his back on drawing; most speculated on where his future illustrations might lead him. The first was written by his early champion and ally, Gleeson White, for the *Magazine of Art* in March 1899. The second was by Mabel Cox for *The Artist*, 1898; and finally the third was by Charles Kains-Jackson for *The Book-Lover's Magazine* in 1908. These three articles are reprinted below as key documents in the study of Laurence Housman's artistic and literary career.

A word must be said about their authors and how each article fit into Housman's critical reputation. Undoubtedly his greatest debt was to G.W.Gleeson White (1851-1898), who first acknowledged his early book designs. As an editor and book designer as well as a major figure in the Arts and Crafts movement, and a devoted historian of the art of the book, his patronage and critical attention were invaluable. He was the author of *English Illustration: The Sixties*, 1897, which remains a standard work, and had served as associate editor of the New York based *The Art-Amateur* from 1891-92, before editing *The Studio*. There he sought out new illustrators, like Aubrey Beardsley, and wrote about their work with skill and perception; as Walter Crane pointed out, White's "quick sympathy and recognition...extended to all young and promising designers of black and white".

Gleeson White discovered Laurence Housman during his duties as the editor and book reviewer of *The Studio*. He continued to promote his work elsewhere, notably as co-editor, with Charles Shannon, of *The Pageant*. He was fond of including Housman's illustrations in his reviews, or in the *Studio Special Number* volumes he produced. Just before his death on 19 October 1898, he had published "Children's Books and their Illustrators", *Studio Special Number*, Winter 1897-98, and here included his first assessment of Housman's career as an illustrator: "Mr Laurence Housman is more than an illustrator of fairy-tales; he is himself a rare creator of such fancies, and has, moreover, an almost unique power of conveying his ideas in the medium. His 'Farm in Fairyland' and 'A House of Joy'...have often been referred to in *The Studio*. Yet, at the risk of reiterating what nobody of taste doubts, one must place his work in this direction head and shoulders above the crowd – even the crowd of excellent illustrators – because its amazing fantasy and caprice are supported by cunning technique that makes the whole work a 'picture', not merely a decoration or an interpretation of the text. As a spinner of entirely bewitching stories, that hold a child spell-bound, and can be read and re-read by adults, he is a near rival of Andersen himself."[10]

A year later his posthumously published survey of Housman the illustrator appeared in the *Magazine of Art*. Of the three articles reprinted here, this was the only one written with Housman's advice and supervision. It is an enthusiastic survey which a future editor tempers with his own editorial comment, pointing out Housman's obvious weaknesses which Gleeson White overlooked ("his shadow lines, which he carries lengthways with the limb he is drawing, and even with the torso... Bodies drawn in this way look limp and flabby."). This same editor concludes that at the age of thirty-four, Housman was too young for a full assessment of his illustrative powers, as Gleeson White had tried to do.

A more objective survey of Housman's book illustrations appeared in *The Artist* in 1898. This London-based magazine, then in its eighteenth year, published Mabel Cox's glowing, uncritical tribute, which echoed Gleeson White's admiration of Housman's versatility. She began with an extravagant claim: "There is probably no artist whose work is more difficult to approach, for purely critical purposes, than Laurence Housman." She added he defied categorization (a remark which surely delighted Housman): "He has the vigour to be himself." But in the end, like the *Magazine of Art* editor, she agreed it was too early to fully assess his career. Only one thing was clear: "His work may change in method, but it can never become more individual." It is an example of the quality of breathless admiration Housman could command among journalists, however untrained their artistic or literary tastes.

Before the appearance of the third critical piece, in 1908, Housman's illustrations and book designs appeared in various publications of "modern" design. Esther Wood's survey, "Modern Book Bindings and their Designers", a *Studio Special Number*, Winter 1899-1900, included Housman's cover designs alongside the work of Granville Fell, Charles Robinson, F.D.Bedford, Alice B.Woodward, Talwin Morris, and especially Charles Ricketts. The author believed Ricketts and Housman alone "represent a more robust and virile imagination working through individualities strongly distinct, both from the preceeding designers and from each other". But above all, Housman's bindings, with their pure, rich ornament were most "strongly composed and congruous with the temperament of the author". She went on to offer the first analysis of how Housman's style affected the viewer: "It is in this vein that Laurence Housman's work becomes most satisfying to the mind and eyes. In figure drawing his power verges continually on the grotesque – as perfevid, convulsive, riotous, and restless almost as that of Blake; but, as with so many on whose spirit the burden of romantic feeling presses hard, it is in the beauty of the earth itself that the heavy and the weary weight, the burden of the mystery is lighted; and

by the choice and use of the natural forms a richly sensuous fancy attunes itself more perfectly to artistic ends." She concluded Housman was a "decorative symbolist"; and was "seeking beauty supremely, but pursuing it by devious and fanciful ways, mystic, suggestive, and full of intellectual motive and idea".

His technical accomplishments as a pen draughtsman were stressed by *The Studio* critic who attended the Private View of his farewell drawings exhibition at the Fine Art Society in October 1901. "The perfect harmony of the masses of fine detail in Mr Housman's drawings is a grace so easy to miss, that one cannot enjoy it without thinking of the perils it has passed through. For this reason, to an extent more or less obvious, its appeal is

Housman's preoccupation with surface detail occasionally obscured the figures and led to confusion, here "The Prince with the Nine Sorrows", from
The House of Joy, *1895.*

made as a *tour de force*, somewhat to its injury as a refinement of subtle art... It is not, then, from a technical point of view that Mr Housman is most admirable, though many seem glad to miss his real worth as a creative illustrator of subtle and original charm, in order that they may bestow a petting admiration upon the fastidious skill displayed by his spider-webbing in pen-craftmanship." This admiration for his technical virtuosity with a pen led J.M.Bulloch to include Housman's subtle pen drawing, "The Japanese Kite" (from *The Blue Moon*), in his "Modern Pen Drawings, European and American", *Studio Special Number*, Winter, 1901. Here Bulloch praised the delicate penwork shading, where Housman "managed to

---

*"The Japanese Kite" to
"The Way of the Wind", from* The Blue Moon, *1904. The intricate ink work was praised by* The Studio *in 1901.*

reproduce by the pen the best side of the wood-engraver's art at first hand".

By the turn of the century Housman's drawings appealed to the collector's market, and some had appeared at the Loan Exhibition of Modern Illustration in 1900 at the Victoria and Albert Museum, where they were admired by a new generation of art students. The collectors were given the first list of his book illustrations in R.E.D. Sketchley's *English Book Illustration of To-day*, 1903, where over two full pages were devoted to his style. Sketchley also reproduced double-page the frontispiece and title opening to *The Field of Clover*, and ironically this, *The Studio* reviewer claimed, had saved Sketchley's book – praiseworthy only for its "specimens of the wonderful wood-engravings of Laurence Housman". Sketchley's own claims for Housman linked him with Crane, Heywood Sumner, Anning Bell, Millais, Furniss, and "other clever draughtsmen". But he added, "Mr Laurence Housman stands alone among modern illustrators", although his influences were numerous: the Sixties School, Ricketts and Shannon, Dürer, Blake, Calvert. And yet his style was "all that is his own": "Of a talent that treats always of enchanted places, where 'reality' is a long day's journey down a dusty road, it is difficult to speak without suggesting that it is all just a charming dalliance with pretty fancies, lacking strength. Of the strength of Mr Housman's imagination, however, his work speaks." In the end, Sketchley found his style was totally unified: "The words belong to the pictures, the pictures to the words."

It was this consideration, linking Housman's literary work with his drawings, which lies at the core of the third critical assessment article reprinted here. It was written by Charles Kains-Jackson, literary critic for the short-lived Scottish book collector magazine, *The Book-Lover's Magazine* in 1908. Kains-Jackson was in fact Housman's friend, whom he called that "funny little Kains-Jackson" and loved for his entertaining visits filled with "scandalous tittle-tattle".[11] They shared outspoken views on homosexuality (Kains-

Jackson lost his post as editor of the homoerotic *Artist and Journal of Home Culture* in 1894 for "New Chivalry", advocating male friendships beyond ordinary marriage). On the strength of this kinship, Kains-Jackson set out to investigate Housman the writer as well as illustrator. His article was again less critical, more a tribute to his friend's versatility. Like Gleeson White and Mabel Cox, he was overwhelmed by Housman's versatility, and foundered for his own labels. He dismissed the current "epicurean ascetic" category, and believed there was greater significance in Housman's themes. "Is he in art and letters the man of the morrow?" He incorporated artistic influences and gave excerpts from the poems and plays in an elegant and skilfully woven tapestry of his literary and artistic accomplishments. It remains a valuable study of Housman's career by a perceptive contemporary, who was himself aware of Housman's strengths and weaknesses as "poet-artist, a professional exponent of not one, but two of the fine arts. This for moderns has the stimulus of surprise."

Laurence Housman's critical reputation in America was based upon occasional reviews in the more exclusive literary journals and the publication there of some of his early illustrated editions and book designs for John Lane, when he found the American publishers for them. His first illustrated book to appear in the American bookshops was *Jump to Glory Jane,* Macmillans ordering 250 copies from Harry Quilter for distribution in America. But John Lane was most responsible for introducing Housman's book designs to publishers in Boston, Chicago and New York. These were eventually reviewed in influential literary papers like *The Bookman* (where Housman's Chantry drawing to Kipling's verse appeared as late as 1906), and the New York based *The Critic,* known in London as "the first literary journal in America". A powerful voice through its topical columns of the current publishing world, *The Critic* reviewed Housman's books in its "London Letter", "Boston Letter" or "Chicago Letter" columns, where the latest John Lane title was acknowledged and occasionally given a substantial notice.

But reviews were sporadic and in the end failed to establish Housman in America as an influential artist of the book. American audiences objected to his grotesque figures, the rarefied themes, the exaggerated realism, and confused symbols which failed to appeal to their more conservative tastes. It took four years alone for *The Field of Clover* to find an American publisher. And even when John Lane secured American publishers for his new Housman designed books, sales were always disappointingly low.[12] Indeed, it is fair to say Housman as an artist was never fully appreciated in America. His reputation there was made by his writing, especially from the overwhelming success of *An Englishwoman's Love-Letters*, which was heavily pirated and extravagantly reviewed in American papers. But even this kind of popular recognition proved valuable when, on Housman's first visit to America in 1916, he was accepted and warmly welcomed on his lecture tour to declare his firm support of the League of Nations.

In Britain by the 1920s, his illustrated story collections had been long out of print. But there was sufficient interest in his fantasies for anthologies of the best of his stories to be published as *A Doorway in Fairyland* and *Moonshine and Clover*, both in 1922. They also appeared in American editions. Fortunately the stories were still linked with their original illustrations, for this was the unique aspect of Housman's contribution to fairy literature. When *The Studio* reprinted "The Traveller's Shoes" (his delicate ink drawing from *A Doorway in Fairyland*) in a new Special Number, "British Book Illustration. Yesterday and Today", Winter, 1923-24, the drawing was heralded as an example of Housman's inimitable style: "Mr Laurence Housman, being imaginatively expressive in pictorial as well as literary art, has had the advantage of illustrating his own stories, and, since he has written some very beautiful and original stories and some with a quaint fancy, his illustrative faculty has been charmingly responsive."

It was perhaps unavoidable that later

Beardsley, Charles Condor, Charles Rick-etts". Such distinctions minimalized his individuality, and were the basis for Housman's own distrust of critical labels and influences. Holbrook Jackson went on, for example, to explain Housman was just one of several artists who, after Beardsley, had fallen under the spell of William Morris and Charles Ricketts. Even more specialist critics and historians, like Forrest Reid, author of *Illustrators of the Sixties*, 1928, claimed Housman merely followed in the well-worn footsteps of Walter Crane and Burne-Jones (who worked with Morris). He was a competent artist of the book, who took "the book itself into consideration; designing initial letters and working out elaborate borders and title pages". But again these were largely artists of the Nineties, the labels and influences steeped in the mustiness of familiarity, rather than innovation.

Indeed it was not until the mid 1960s that Housman's true influence and innovations were recognized. John Russell Taylor in his *The Art Nouveau Book in Britain*, 1966, devoted several pages to his importance as a book designer. He claimed Housman had developed "a highly individual, completely recognizable style, and remained true to it throughout his fairly brief career as a book designer". Most importantly, he had perfected the use of various formats in book design; an innovation Taylor traced to the experimental book designs of the Nonesuch Press of Sir Francis Meynell.

Laurence Housman's versatility, the fact he abandoned his artistic career after so short a period, and still produced such a prolific number of books, articles, novels, plays and lectures, proved a severe detriment to his reputation as a book designer and illustrator. He in fact made little mention of this aspect of his professional life in his autobiography; and none at all in his own obituary. Consequently when he died in 1959, *The Times* dismissed his drawings in one sentence, as does the *Dictionary of National Biography* in its own sizeable entry. His work is only briefly noted in the more current surveys of illustration, notably by Ruari McLean in *Victorian Book Design*, 1972 and Percy Muir's *Victorian Illustrated Books*, 1971, which linked him with his Victorian predecessors, but failed to acknowledge his innovations. As Laurence predicted, as a writer he was largely overshadowed by his more famous brother; and he and Clemence did not receive proper recognition for their artistic careers until "The Housmans" exhibition of their drawings, engravings and books at the National Book League in London in 1975. Then, for a brief period, reviewers and critics began a re-assessment of their influence. And it was, and remains, a substantial achievement. According to a recent catalogue of a collection of Housman's work, Laurence produced over 600 literary and artistic pieces of work alone.[13] It is hoped that the present volume will go some way towards redressing the balance, and help to establish Laurence Housman and Clemence, his creative sister, as the artists of imagination and influence they undoubtedly were.

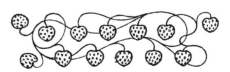

Tailpiece from Goblin Market, *1893.*

REPRINTED ARTICLES

Magazine of Art, March 1899.
THE WORK OF LAURENCE HOUSMAN.

By the late GLEESON WHITE.

THE art of Mr. Laurence Housman is not quite easy to assess, for he has the felicity of expression in two mediums—"pictures" and "words," and a happy knack of combining both utterances in the telling of stories which hold the reader spellbound. The last phrase may be taken literally, as then it becomes evident that those who fall under the spell cannot obviously pose as impartial critics. Hence it were best to abandon any attempt at delivering judgment, and recount Mr. Housman's achievements as impassively as possible, although such an effort to act as an unprejudiced onlooker savours of ingratitude when the pleasure Mr. Housman has afforded one comes to memory.

To appreciate fully Mr. Housman's drawings it is necessary to be acquainted with his poems and stories, not because his pictures are drawn chiefly from subjects of his own invention, but because in his writings it is even more easy to recognise the curious realism of his imaginings. He achieves this end in a way not wholly unrelated to the realistic manner of Defoe, by naïve, trivial, and apparently irrelevant details, that recall at once the method of "Robinson Crusoe" and the discursive style of the old balladists. Yet the result is by no means sham antique. He strings you together neither forged curios nor (to use Mr. Aymer Vallance's clever portmanteau-word) "spurios." No one could call his style Wardour Street English; yet, with a deft use of unexpected words and crisp, racy sentences, he preserves the other-worldliness of Romance, avoiding all the while both the sham archaic no less than the cheap pathetic.

THE COUNCIL.
From "The Land of Elfintown." By Permission of Messrs. Macmillan and Co.

In his drawings an academic critic might perhaps be annoyed to learn that the artist first completes his design and then compares it with the "life" model, deliberately preserving certain lapses from truth, should he feel that the sentiment and decorative value of his composition will be more fully realised thereby. Without affirming that this is an example which students should take as a precedent, one also must not forget the old precept, that genius consists in breaking rules. Although it would be an unfriendly act to call Mr. Housman a genius—even by implication — yet a candid admirer must own that the elusive charm of many designs is not vitally lessened because their anatomy is perverted. There is a time for undiluted candour and a time for playful equivocation; but, unless the latter be deliberately put forward as the former, the least casuistical person may forgive the perversion.

The fact must be faced that sentiment—even to the extent of false sentiment and rank sentimentality—plays an important part in life and in art. Nor must it be forgotten that the sentiment which looks affected to those it fails to move, may be true enough to others. The fantastic designs by William Blake are accepted as inspired creations by many critics well informed and sane, men who would not forgive any errors of proportion or inept "drawing" in other pictures. So the intense "soulfulness" of Rossetti is a by-word for the many to scoff at, and the vivid delight of the few. The most honest course is surely to try to put one's self in touch with the artist, and if he impress you to own it without prejudice, careless of ridicule, whether it take the form of abuse or grovelling admiration. It were folly to compare work like Mr. Housman's with that, say, of Arthur Boyd Houghton, Randolph Caldecott, or Sir John Gilbert; one of these illustrators may satisfy your critical judgment most fully, another may be more obedient to tradition, a third may impress by his animal spirits and sheer vitality. But to say therefore that only the one is good and the rest bad, is folly. In calling Mr. Housman's method realistic—the word is used only for his method, and by no means for his subjects —it is the matter-of-fact narrative of impossible incidents which witches a listener, and the same applies, in a less degree possibly, to imaginative illustration.

The designs of Arthur Boyd Houghton which have been the objects of Mr. Housman's eulogy are often "realistic" in subject, but they are not realistic in their treatment. His American sketches of actual people and incidents are not literal records of the customs of the United States; but even at their most grotesque they convey something far more emotional than the actual scene, and give you not the reflection as in a mirror, but the impression of the scene on one observer coloured by his prejudice and his mental bias, tricked with his whimsy, and translated in a literary composition to express his own idiom.

So Mr. Housman puts his fancies on paper, and builds up by picture and phrase a world that never was, wherein the motives that inspire actual humanity are transfigured or burlesqued to suit his purpose. That he conceals the too-

obvious moral, exactly as he hides too-apparent imitation, is not necessarily to his discredit. The gnomes and princesses, the goblins and weird

FRONTISPIECE TO "THE FIELD OF CLOVER."
By Permission of Messrs. Kegan Paul, Trench and Co.

women, are but puppets wherewith he plays you a masque that is as unreal as an old miracle play and at times no less based upon the noblest motives.

From the first he has struck out a line for himself and swerved not. That Mr. Charles Ricketts was, and is, his avowed hero is

THE WORK OF LAURENCE HOUSMAN. 201

apparent enough. Yet it would be unfair to either to exaggerate the debt; and time has shown that of the two artists, both still young, each

TITLE-PAGE TO "THE FIELD OF CLOVER."
By Permission of Messrs. Kegan Paul, Trench and Co.

has already developed his own manner, so that to-day the likeness is very far removed. Indeed, the real similarity is much less than a casual observer would suspect. You have but to compare Mr. Ricketts' examples of conventional design with those by Mr. Housman—say a typical book-cover by each—to find absolutely essential

divergences. The one nervous, emotional, and exquisitely personal; the other, complex it may be, but under perfect control, and although individual, yet with distinct recognition of certain established precedents. It is needless to set the drawings of each in rivalry; for if anyone thinks the pictures in "All-Fellows" very like those in "Hero and Leander," no argument to the contrary would be likely to convince an observer so careless.

Forgetting, in deference to their author's attitude towards them, certain drawings in the short-lived "Universal Review," the first designs Mr. Housman published were those to "Jump to Glory Jane," by George Meredith, which Mr. Harry Quilter issued in a separate volume. In these we find full evidence of a personal expression, even if immature. The bizarre legend is depicted grotesquely, as it should be, but also seriously; you do not laugh at the jumping saint, even if a smile of tolerance is forced from you. The pathetic aspect of a sect only one degree more crazy than the one hundred and forty-four listed in Whitaker's Almanack is so sympathetically treated that you feel a certain respect for its eccentric effort towards perfection. The Mormon subjects by Boyd Houghton impress one as inspired by critical satire rather than by amused tolerance; it is as if Houghton saw only the pitiful absurdity of the unbalanced religiosity, and forgot that even this is only a vulgarised effort to overcome the "world, the flesh, and the devil." It is just because Mr. Housman, despite his paradox and satire, reveals a curiously insistent tolerance, combined with insistent hatred of all selfishness and pain, that you are tempted to reckon him among the preachers. If this be true, he occupies a position almost unique just now. The man who believes that art for art's

THE MOONFLOWER.

From "The House of Joy." By Permission of Messrs. Kegan Paul, Trench and Co.

sake is sufficient, and he who thinks that art is but the handmaid to morals, are both plentiful enough; but those who believe that art is a great force, with its own message to the world to impart in its own way, are few in all countries.

If "Jump to Glory Jane" is solemn underneath its satire, "Goblin Market," Christina Rossetti's poem, which was the next published, is wholly in the spirit of the work. Knowing Mr. Housman's devotion to the art of Dante Gabriel Rossetti, and remembering the frontispiece and title-page to the earlier edition of the work, it is surprising to find how little he has imitated "Buy from us with Golden Curl" or "Golden Head by Golden Head," the two designs in question. He has kept the bird-and-cat-like aspect of the goblins, but he has clothed the

figures with smocks and flapping hats, so that they have a grotesqueness of their own and are far less animal than the Rossetti originals. On the other hand "Lama of the Golden Locks" is no longer a Rossetti damozel, but a country wench in a sun-bonnet, who seems not wholly unrelated to "Jumping Jane." In this book the sweeping movement of the main lines, no less than the purely conventional devices which decorate its type-pages, reveal Mr. Housman himself, not more a disciple of Dante Gabriel Rossetti's than of Mr. Ricketts', and owing little to either except a certain intensity common to the work of both. The dainty little edition of "Goblin Market"—perhaps the most charmingly bound volume, with the single exception of "Silverpoints," that has yet been issued by any publisher—is not inaccessible, so that here it will be unnecessary to describe its illustrations or to discuss its decorations—pleasant conceits in figures and devices which do not disturb the mental pictures called up by the poem, but rather suggest more fantastic images than the average reader would be likely to imagine for himself. This is surely the more true method of illustrating poetry: to "fill my lady's missal marge with flowrets" instead of interleaving complete pictures that conflict in direct rivalry with the poet's word-painting. The same year (1893) saw the publication of "Weird Tales," with illustrations by Mr. Housman, a work upon which the artist sets no particular value.

In 1894, "The Land of Elfintown" by Jane Barlow, was issued by Messrs. Macmillan in a volume not wholly unlike "Goblin Market;" but if in outward aspect it recalls the other, the spirit of its illustrations is quite unlike. These are more clearly influenced by Mr. Charles Ricketts, and more "passion-fraught." Indeed, they have provoked some critics to employ the adjective "morbid," which is a blessed word good people who are puzzled hurl, as a last resort, against much in art which is for the time incomprehensible to them. As you study these designs and recognise again their singular charm, the probable criticism of the average Briton occurs to you, and you find why it has been uttered. There is no doubt that in drawing and in conception they are singularly unlike the conventions of the fairy-land as popularly presented, and that the figures are strangely unlike those of Sir Noel Paton or the old-time Christmas card. So one may find the "Ride of the Valkyrie" and the "Tannhäuser" Overture unlike the "Midsummer Night's Dream" music. Possibly the simpler convention is most satisfying to those who take fairy-land to be a sort of glorified nursery, "full of good little people" who keep their pinafores clean and behave with conscious rectitude. But

THE WORK OF LAURENCE HOUSMAN.

203

the legends of pixies and elves are almost always impregnated by an uncanny, unholy mystery; and that Mr. Housman materialises the nebulous beings with some of these qualities is perhaps the secret of his success in "thrilling" other people not easily moved by modern fairy stories.

Perhaps, however, these feelings are provoked not so much by Mr. Housman's pictures as by his two volumes of original stories—"A Farm in Fairyland" (1894) and "A House of Joy" (1894).

The title-pages of these two books demand a special word. In both appear most elaborately interwoven borders of interlaced strap-work, which reveals Mr. Housman's sure mastery of line; yet this elaborate framing does not crush either of the four pictures which are sheer marvels of craft, so delicate in their line and crowded with intricate pattern, that the elaborate borders seem simple by comparison. Drawn very slightly larger than they appear in the reproduction, it seems barely possible that the complex and exquisitely minute detail could be achieved by ordinary eyesight. Yet, as a matter of fact, they were; and when asked how the delicate minuteness of these could be set down without a magnifying glass, Mr. Housman laughingly replied, "I think I have eyes at the tips of my fingers, I seem to feel the line even if I can hardly see it." It is worth noting that these decorative pages in "black-and-white," produced when the "Aubrey Beardsley" style was in the air, reveal not the slightest trace of his influence, an influence which can be discovered in the work of dozens who believe they dislike it no less than in others—the American, W. H. Bradley, for instance—who are obvious disciples. It is possible that some of the charm of the illustrations to these books is reflected from the many inventions in prose that they depict. So fascinating are these that to quote largely were well nigh irresistible, but, all the same, the temptation cannot be obeyed. Only, if there be any lovers of pure phantasy and graceful conceit who do not know these delightful stories, one envies the pleasure that still awaits them. Although both volumes were, I believe, produced under the author's direction, and are singularly comely pieces of bookbinding, they are not decorated in any sense.

The initial letters are his own, and extremely charming, but, beyond pleasantly proportioned margins and excellently placed typography, the style of each does not differ noticeably from the work of any

good publisher. This may show that in the "get-up" of the printed book Mr. Ricketts and Mr. Housman do not follow the same path, sympathetic though each may be to the ideals of the other.

A series of illustrations to a very powerful tale, "The Were-Wolf," by the artist's sister, Miss Clemence Housman, appeared in the same year as the "House of Joy." This was followed by "Green Arras," a book of original poems by Mr. Housman, with another of his elaborate double title-pages whereon the borders are even more complex and the details of the panels still more marvellously wrought than in the two fairy-books. *To say that these title-pages stand absolutely alone, and that no other artist, living or dead, has done work like them, is mere fact;*

FRONTISPIECE TO "THE SENSITIVE PLANT."
By Permission of Messrs. Dent and Co.

to add that no living artist could beat them in the fastidiously delicate embroidery of their pen-work, is a statement one may risk with a light heart. Yet they are not without breadth and largeness of design; and if you wish it gained with less effort you have but to turn to the end-papers to find it. In the full-page drawings we have many a glimpse of landscape treated

These are not mere transcripts of daily life; but a transfigured presentation of common objects that are seen under circumstances of supernatural, or at least highly-strung, emo-tions. Charged with his weakness of Nature, Mr. Housman takes refuge in a pleasant paradox. "Nature is not a fit subject for art, but may be a very useful medium," he exclaims with a grave

THE MERCIFUL DRAUGHT.
From "All-Fellows." By Permission of Messrs. Kegan Paul, Trench and Co.

in a way no pen-draughtsman to-day seems to attempt. Perhaps "The Corn-keeper," a new version of the design which first appeared with its accompanying poem in " Atalanta," might be taken as one entirely typical example of the artist's manner were you limited to the choice of a single work. In it one feels that the men of the 'sixties, the figures of A. Boyd Houghton, and the landscapes of J. W. North have their legitimate descendant; while at the same time it has a certain intensity not to be found in the earlier work, and perhaps a certain " preciousness " which may or may not be deemed an advance on the earlier school. This possible objection is mooted not to traverse such an opinion but merely to declare if it be well founded; yet it is due most probably in great part to the themes which attract the artist.

reasonableness that might mystify one who did not know his keen sense of humour.

With " All-Fellows "—another book of fan-tasy which those who love regard too deeply to attempt to analyse publicly, containing some of his most matured illustrations—and " Gods and their Makers " (1897), a volume published with-out illustrations, the list of books for which he is responsible must close.

This, however, leaves his bindings without a word. Yet, although they require a separate article even to do them scant justice, it must not be forgotten that, from the large paper edi-tion of Mr. Harry Quilter's "Preferences" to the wrapper for "The Commonwealth," he has pro-duced a series which collectors prize and foreign-ers carry back as examples of the supremacy of English bookbinding.

THE WORK OF LAURENCE HOUSMAN. 205

The clever and beautiful designs in gold tracery for "Goblin Market," "Elfintown," "Green Arras," "The Viol of Love," and "Elizabethan Sonnet Cycles" are examples of pure pattern without figures. In another class are "The House of Joy," "A Farm in Fairyland," and "Jump to Glory Jane;" while a third list would include Francis Thompson's "Poems" and "Sister Songs," "Cuckoo Songs" by Katharine Tynan, "Love in Idleness" by Marion Crawford, "The Flower of the Mind," Mrs. Meynell's new anthology, "A Pomander of Verse" by E. Nesbit, "Spikenard," "The Were-Wolf," all of which, if less complex, are hardly less characteristic.

Nor should book-plates for A. W. Pollard, Hannah Brace, Robert and Evelyn Benson, and H. Bland be forgotten, any more than Mr. Housman's contribution to "The Pageant," "The Parade," "Bibliographica," or his monograph on Boyd Houghton; for all these show different phases of his personality.

Yet with an artist still young, as the outside world reckons, and a mere baby—for Mr. Housman is still far off half the allotted age of man—as politicians would rank him, it would be foolish to attempt a *catalogue raisonné* of his work. Still more futile would it be to estimate his future place in art; for his complex manner and subtle perception of emotions the reverse of commonplace will most likely keep him a limited, if cultured, audience. Yet, as "Gods and their Makers" has shown, at any moment his parable in words or devices may become appreciated by the public; and even popularity in the widest sense may be one of the dangers in store. Here nothing has been said of his scholastic training; for with so vividly personal a manner, it is of little consequence whose advice he has disregarded or what rules he has broken. Nor has his method of work been touched upon; for his rapid, nervous sketches and studies, full of power as they are, are not suggestions of the finished drawing, and are wrought with a loose line and rapid handling that, in the nature of things, would fail to express all that he wants them to express finally. It is good to think that all our weavers of fiction and designers of pictures and pattern are not of his kind, for piquant odours and flavours are more lovable when they are also rare; and yet still more good to feel that Britain has once more the sole possession of a few that are beginning to attract not only the curiosity but the envy of Continental critics. For the test of importance in art is that a man should convince you that his way of seeing Nature through his temperament is both new and interesting. If he can do this with technical sufficiency, it is quite a secondary matter what peculiar aspects of art may attract his experiments; for by his witchery, once you fall under it, they will attract you also and cause you to re-formulate all your canons of criticism hitherto in force, that he may not be left outside the pale.

"A Field of Clover." By Laurence Housman. With illustrations by the Author, engraved by Clemence Housman. (Kegan Paul and Co. 1898.)

NOTE.—Although a young man, Mr. Housman bids fair to take his place as the artist who, at the beginning of the twentieth century, occupied a place midway between Rossetti and William Morris on the one hand, and A. B. Houghton and Mr. C. Ricketts on the other. We do not mean to say that he has yet revealed a genius equal to the greatest of these, but genius in some degree he undoubtedly has, whether as an artist or as a writer. He has fancy, designs charmingly, draws beautifully when he chooses, with a sentiment which, if somewhat "precious," is instinct with a quality of art that to many must be irresistible. We deal with Mr. Housman's work so fully in the late Mr. Gleeson White's article that we need say little more in general praise. We would, however, point out a defect with which he taints some of his work; not that wherein he follows Houghton. We refer to his shadow lines, which he usually carries lengthways with the limb he is drawing, and even with the torso. He certainly gains some quality by what appears after all a mannerism, but loses his anatomical construction. Bodies drawn in this way look limp and flabby. A word of high praise should be accorded to the fine work of the graver here shown; we are not surprised that Mr. Housman dedicates his book, as he prettily does, "To my dear wood-engraver." The borders are charming but not entirely perfect.

THE BOOK-ILLUSTRATIONS OF LAURENCE HOUSMAN.

From "GOBLIN MARKET
*(By permission, Messrs.
Macmillan & Co.)*

THERE is probably no artist whose work is more difficult to approach, for purely critical purposes, than Laurence Housman. As poet, artist or designer, his train of thought is always definitely personal and peculiar, and his work is not always for him who runs to read—a characteristic which is not necessarily the mark of an artist ; but it has a second characteristic which is the mark of an artist, for the more we study it the more we get from it.

Laurence Housman was not an infant prodigy. Until out of his teens he did nothing to show more than average talent. His "art education" was of the most ordinary kind, and although during it he carried off some prizes and medals, he produced nothing really exceptional. The first real influence he felt was that of Blake ; Dürer, also, was an early and undoubted influence. It was while studying Blake for a critical essay that he first realized the possibility of breaking away from academic rules of perfect anatomical drawing, for the sake of obtaining spirited expression.

As a result of this development, he published, in the "Universal Review," his "Green Gaffer," with his own illustrations. This was seen by Charles Ricketts, who sought out and greatly encouraged the young artist. Ricketts, together with C. H. Shannon, commended his escape from academic rule, and persuaded him to keep on his own path, with the courage of his own opinions, and to let feeling supersede technique. Housman's next production was the

FROM " GREEN ARRAS."   LAURENCE HOUSMAN.
(By permission of Mr. John Lane.)

illustration of " Jump to Glory Jane," by George Meredith. He gladly accepted an offer to do this, feeling that its unusual bizarre note would give him his opportunity. Blundering in technique as it is, and at times almost ludicrous in drawing, he has never done anything more vigorously expressive ; his critics, even when unfavourable, all allowed that his work was almost marvellously in key with the poem.

By this attempt the artist realized once and for all that it was possible to get a thorough grip of a subject, in spite of limitations of technique ; that the former is infinitely more important than technical facility.

Then came the rather difficult task of finding subjects. He was offered the chance of illustrating "Weird Tales from Northern Seas," a translation from Jonas Lie, and this was published in 1893, appearing about the same time as the edition of Christina Rossetti's "Goblin Market," which Housman asked and obtained permission to illustrate. In this he again succeeded in grasping the spirit of the poem, and the drawings are of a highly imaginative order ; there is a wealth of decorative detail such as Housman has never surpassed in charm, whatever he may since then have gained in facility.

A little later Housman began to take seriously to writing. In 1894 "A Farm in Fairyland," and the next year "The House of Joy" appeared. They are collections of the purest and most delightful fairy tales, with his own illustrations. About the same time he illustrated "The Werewolf," by his sister, Miss Clemence Housman ; and later appeared the volume of poems "Green Arras," followed by a book of legends in prose and verse entitled "All Fellows," both illustrated. A critical monograph on the work of Houghton, an artist whose influence is very apparent in much of Housman's work, was published a little later. "Gods and their Makers," an unillustrated story, although his latest publication, is one of his earliest efforts in literature, and its appearance has caused some dissatisfaction to certain of his admirers.

An important branch of Housman's work which must be mentioned, although we are

FROM "GOBLIN MARKET."   L. HOUSMAN.

(*By permission of Messrs. Macmillan & Co.*)

unity to his thought; that is practically all that technique has done for him. His figures are still "incorrect," but Housman's "incorrectness" has been growing more graceful, more serviceable to the impression he wishes to convey.

If an artist has not got logical grip of his own ways of thought, art training and technical facility are positive dangers to him. It is easy to learn by receipt to produce "pretty" work, but prettiness is the main obstacle on the road to beauty—for this, if for no other reason, that prettiness tends to lack of individuality; it is the typical mark of things mostly foolish. Beauty, on the other hand, is character; is, as Walt Whitman says, "blood and brain"; more beauty lies dormant in what is rugged and strenuous than in what is "correct" and conventional. This is exactly what people whose minds are outside the reach of artistic feeling cannot understand. They cannot see that the work of Giotto has in it visible beauty of the first rank, that Dürer is one of the greatest masters of beauty that has ever lived; they will tell you, when they are honest, that Dürer and Giotto are ugly; they will show you where Dürer "goes wrong in his anatomy."

unfortunately unable to include it in our illustrations, is the drawing of book-plates. He has not done a great number, but several are of rare beauty and merit.

As regards Housman's development, from "Jump to Glory Jane" to "Green Arras" is assuredly a long way, at any rate from a technical point of view. He has chosen to feel his way along his own path rather than be led by others, and to discover for himself the secret of beauty. He found, as others have found, that too much art training and too much drawing from the life and study of anatomy resulted in loss of feeling; that they, instead of helping him to say what he wanted to say, caused his work to smack of the model. Therefore he dropped life studies, forgot his anatomy, and determined to draw no more than he felt, however much he blundered and stammered before he acquired his full power of self-expression. Now that his handling of his work is so much finer, since he has gained complete control over the point of his pen, his drawings are less open to accidental disfigurements; he is able to embellish his main theme with beauty of detail and to give more pictorial

FROM "GOBLIN MARKET."   L. HOUSMAN.

(*By permission of Messrs. Macmillan & Co.*)

Now what we need to realize is that the artist and the poet do not want to see literally. In art a figure may be just as far removed from the flesh as poetry is from the language of everyday life; the work of both artist and poet artists limit their love to the visible things of nature; in others it goes to the hidden, the invisible, and becomes what we call ideal. The artist puts beautiful ideas into form, so that within the world he creates they become facts.

"THE THREE KINGS."
FROM "GREEN ARRAS."

LAURENCE HOUSMAN.

(*By permission of Mr. John Lane.*)

should be transported from the everyday materials out of which each makes his medium. The artist draws the things he loves; it entirely depends on his love what he draws. Some

The root idea of Laurence Housman's work seems to be that the visible world is a mask of disparity hiding a concealed unity; that the literal acceptance of what the senses tell us is a

FROM " ALL FELLOWS."   L. HOUSMAN.

(By permission of Messrs. Kegan Paul & Co.)

that his figures can step out of their frames into everyday life, that his trees can be blown by the winds of earth; he wishes them to appear and remain improbable to those who cannot see into fairyland with their mind's eye. Thus to many people his work is and will be a dead letter. Not so to children; they, with the profound wisdom of their open minds, follow him one and all delightedly. So it might be with all. Any one who will take the trouble to follow him may gain entry into that world of ideals without which, in some form or other, the meanest and most sordid of us cannot live.

Critics would do well, as soon as they have discovered mastery in a man's work, to follow the maxim of letting his mannerisms alone. There are those who would rank themselves among artists on the strength of a mannerism alone, but mannerism without mastery is as far beneath criticism as mannerism with mastery is above it. An artist who has attained mastery at any point does not use mannerism to supplant any merit to which he can possibly attain; it may be that mannerism covers as gracefully as possible certain defects inevitable to his tem-

distortion of the inner reality; he takes hold of every visible thing he can, and tries to get out of it by symbol or fable some spirit suggestive of a realism more absolute than that supplied by the senses.

Housman is never satisfied with cold, categorical symbolism of the kind that is put in to fill up corners, but his work is full of conscious symbolism, which he aims at bringing into dramatic unity with his subject. Its use is part of his method of creating for us the world of fairyland, the ideal, legendary world. In the everyday world, symbols, like miracles, are not; but in the fairy world we expect them, and therefore a picture should give us that expectation. Housman's drawings have that touch or atmosphere which leads us to expect a symbolic correspondence between the main theme of the picture and its surroundings. For instance, in " Jump to Glory Jane," in the last picture, the death of Jane, one of the death-bed watchers puffs out a candle in which hangs a shroud, while through the chinks of the door comes the white light of dawn. Again, in " Green Arras," in the picture of a man plotting revenge against his queen, there is a tortoise creeping along the path towards the palace, and in the garden is a scarecrow of the queen herself:—a dramatic summing of the situation.

It is from a visionary world that Housman speaks, through ideal and symbolic art, to the imagination. He would not have us feel

FROM "THE END OF ELFINTOWN."   L. HOUSMAN.

(By permission of Messrs. Macmillan & Co.)

perament. Trust him, if he have once touched beauty in his own way on his own lines, to know better than we can do for him by what means he can best reach his goal. There are those of Housman's admirers who would claim him as a shining light among the "decadents." We fear they do him too much honour! His poetry is often somewhat dismal, it is true, but if he talks of death it is sanely, as of rest; he talks tenderly of and to children, and lovingly of beasts and of "The Earth our Mother"; above all he harps continually on the mystery of growth and birth with a frankness that is worthy of its theme. He does not write or draw anything because it is approved by any little "clique," decadent or otherwise, any more than because it is taught by art schools. He has the vigour to be himself. He is still very young and his work may change in method, but it can never become more individual.

Housman has never really mastered the difficulty of working for process reproduction. In this respect his earliest work is his best;

FROM "THE HOUSE OF JOY."   L. HOUSMAN.

(By permission of Messrs. Kegan Paul & Co.)

for, as his style became finer in treatment, it suffered a correspondingly increasing loss in reproduction. Finding this to be the case, he once made an effort to revert to his earlier and more open style, but abandoned the attempt, as he found he was working against the grain. So far, his work has reproduced best in half-tone, as in "All Fellows," but even there, in spite of the reproduction being admirably done, the drawings suffered an inevitable loss. Thus we can say that the public do not yet know the best of Housman's work as an artist, and this fact lends special interest to his next book of fairy tales, where the illustrations will be wood engravings by his sister, Miss Clemence Housman, for she, as some admirers of her very clever literary work will be surprised to hear, is expert in the craft of wood engraving.

Our illustrations, some of which the courtesy of Mr. Housman's different publishers has enabled us to reproduce, give a fairly comprehensive idea of his work.

MABEL COX.

FROM "A FARM IN FAIRYLAND."   L. HOUSMAN.

Book-Lover's Magazine, 1908.

The Work of Laurence Housman

BY

CHARLES KAINS-JACKSON

EPICUREAN asceticism is the prevailing mark of the culture which is to succeed the Edwardine. Every Pope has his motto, which is also a prophecy, and, even in Protestant lands, coming events cast their epigrams before. A later Victorian æsthete, convicted of applying the morals of Plato to the manners of the masses, might easily have foreseen that the subjects of the next monarch would look forward to Lady Godiva entering Coventry in a motor car. Mr. Housman has been called an epicurean ascetic: is he in art and letters the man of the morrow? Not in our view, because we do not accept the description. A whole stage must be traversed before we come to that which is behind the work of our subject to-day. In order to ascertain what that something is, let us examine the work itself. We shall find epicureanism, we shall hear the ascetic note, but we shall come, I think, to the conclusion, as we proceed, that they are merely part of the way, means to an end; at most, visions to right and left as the artist proceeds on his journey.

Perhaps the first thing which interests his fellow-countrymen in Mr. Laurence Housman is that he is a poet-artist, a professional exponent of not one, but two of the fine arts. This for moderns has the stimulus of surprise. 'Put the sonnet in the frame' is the familiar, if facile, gibe of the smart American. The distrust of more than a single specialised excellence extends to politics. The *Times* leader on Mr. Balfour's speech at Cambridge, when he lectured on the 'Decadent Note in Literature,' was a delightful manifestation of this distrust. 'The lecture was excellent, the politician made the best of lecturers, for while Parliament taught a man to talk, it cured him of any tendency to be didactic.' All the same, the good Balfourian of Printing House Square was most obviously and amusingly uncomfortable. Mr. Housman gave the public a similar thrill when he showed in the *Englishwoman's Love Letters* (London : Murray, 1900) his ability to appreciate a woman's point of view more than anybody but an artist could expect to do. The public accepted Mr. Housman as a man of letters, and here was evidence proving that he was also an artist. The anonymity of this volume was well maintained for a considerable while, but all critics of the best standing were agreed from the first that the writer was a man, and that he was a man who was something over and beyond a writer pure and simple. The artist looks at this matter, we fancy, from a position the reverse of the average man's. Art, it must be remembered also, transcends sex. So convinced is he of the essential unity of the arts, that he is restrained by the direst modesty from discussing the subject, seeing that the innermost feeling of the painter-artist must be of surprise that he is not a musician-artist also, or a poet-artist, or a sculptor-artist. The arts most widely separate surprise by revelations of strange kinship. A first-rate landscape painter instinctively understands architecture ; the poet sees many pictures that he never writes about. Sculpture is intimately influenced by music. To the strains of Apollo's cithara rose Ilion's towers ; and, similarly, Semitic music brought the towers of Jericho to the ground. Mr. Housman in his drawings often manifests the pencil under the spiritual control of some

2 H

other fine art than design ; in a few, art itself appears to be resolved, and we have a hint, a glimpse, of what moves us in all art.

The second attraction felt by the reader and critic is of a singularly independent individuality. As a writer of serious poetry Mr. Housman early felt the influence of Mr. Swinburne. Thus of the dead (*Gods and their Makers*, p. 210) :—

> 'They toil not, they plough not, they sow not ;
> They are wet not with rain nor dew ;
> Our searchings of heart they know not,
> Nor the answer thereto.'

These surely abide ' there, where the good man is not good.'

> ' A too great fire, most unendurable,'

is a blank verse line showing the same influence ; but the natural bent of our subject was in a different direction, and in the great English symbolists of the early seventeenth century are to be found his real companions and soul compeers. Yet even from them he is sharply separate. The wonderful poem in *All Fellows* (p. 54) could not have been written by the best of them, and, of course, *per contra*, Mr. Housman never attains *their* best ; the 'Love' of George Herbert is sweeter, the 'Good Friday' of Crashaw more majestically passionate, than anything from his pen. He has been very little influenced by the Strict Forms which from 1872 to 1895 had so great a vogue. They 'went out' to a great extent with the older æsthetic movement to which the best and most mature work of Mr. Housman is subsequent. Classical metres have not interested him at all, but he has a musician's ear for quantity as well as accent, and this makes his songs admirably fitted for setting.

If the reader should ask for a cycle of serious lyric verse, limiting us to a dozen song-pieces, we might select for this intimate anthology 'The Desire of Life' (*Gods and their Makers*, p. 118), 'Long through the Night' (*Rue*, p. 7), 'Annus Mirabilis' (*Mendicant Rhymes*, p. 8), 'Amid this grave-strewn, flowerless place' (*All Fellows*, p. 54), 'Oh, Face of Music' (*The Little Land*, p. 47), 'Thou the Arrow' (*The Little Land*, p. 53), 'As by the motion of her Arc' (*Rue*, 94), 'The Wood Fairies' (*Mendicant Rhymes*, p. 9), 'The Naming of Love' (*The Little Land*, p. 58), 'The Last Laugh' (*The*

Little Land, p. 77), 'The Corn-Keeper' (*Green Arras*, p. 35), and the last six lines of the play *Prunella*. This list does not embrace religious poetry, where we should perhaps select ' What know ye of the wounds of Christ ? ' (*Rue*, p. 21), 'The Feast of Corpus Christi' (*Spikenard*, p. 8), 'The Fountain of Life' (*Spikenard*, p. 44), 'The Word Expressed' (*Bethlehem*, p. 39), 'I heard on Christmas Night' (*Bethlehem*, p. 41), 'The Maker of the Sun and Moon' (*English Hymnal*, No. 16), 'St. George' (*English Hymnal*, No. 219), 'Love came and said' (*All Fellows*, p. 92), 'Saint and Sinner' (*The Little Land*, p. 70), and 'All Souls' Day' (*Spikenard*, p. 37), as giving a fair idea of the poet. There can, one imagines, be no doubt whatever as to Mr. Housman's position as a religious poet. He belongs here to no minor band, or set, or school, but is as far removed from the poetry of the *People's Hymnal* ('What ! with pipe and tabor fool away the light ? ' etc.) as is that of Newman from Faber, that of Wordsworth from Christopher Wordsworth, to quote, as one should, cases each within its own communion. In the *English Hymnal* of 1907, that memorable collection, Mr. Housman had a not inconsiderable part. Of the four original hymns contributed by him, reference has already been made to the two which we imagine will be included in almost all future hymnals. The hymn for St. Mark's Day bears too obvious traces of the limits imposed by the subject, or perhaps we should say by the frigidity of a northern and tradition-fearing Church. The beautiful and impressive legends linking St. Mark to the great city of Alexandria, and then later to even more famous Venice, are ignored, and the mystery of St. Mark's Eve, which Mr. Housman could have so effectively indicated, is ignored also. The translations of Latin hymns are scholarly, accurate, and informed with the spirit of their originals ; Nos. 229 and 230 are especially felicitous renderings.

The sense of humour, which is very strong in Mr. Housman's narrative, fairly overflows in his drawing, as witness the pot-bellied hobgoblin in the 'Who's Who' of *Goblin Land* as Katchy-Wallah. He tells us how greatly he appreciates Cruikshank's drawing of the 'Farmer's Son riding on the Fox's Brush,' and that he appreciates it because it makes the wonder probable.

The Work of Laurence Housman

It is a miracle of art, this art-thaumaturgy, a species, be it said with all reverence, of incarnation, a bringing of the miraculous being, event, or thing, within the touch of man. Very early in his own career our artist had this power of capturing the improbable in the net of probability, as witness his illustrations to Christina Rossetti's *Goblin Market* (London : Macmillan, 1893). These verifications of the poetess's hypotheses—for they amount to that—are splendid. They realise the life of the small animals *à marveille*. The illustrations which should face pp. 17, 5, 6, 11, and 12 (only they are printed inwards) may be mentioned as peculiarly excellent. This book should become a treasure. 'Puss in Winter' (*The Little Land*, pp. 7-9) is a revelation of the author at his highest in purely imaginative work. We prefer it to his religious best, though there he soars high and knows the heavens of Crashaw and of Donne. This, however, is more elemental. The makers of myth are not dead. The Greeks before Homer who listened to how Orpheus fell in love with Calaïs, the beautiful Wind, and how the winged youth returned his love, would have made the 'Snow-White Cat' a living legend of the hilly lands and little hill towns of Thrace. If Mr. Housman had written nothing besides this story in short lines, it would suffice to give him a lasting place in our literature, seeing that it is not minor poetry, but 'the real thing,' that it is alike in thought and form perfectly original, and that it has what may be called the catholic note of intellect, the real presence of Idea. 'St Peter's Fish' (p. 19), in the same remarkable and little-known volume, is broader in its humour, quite unforgettable when once read.

The fantastic poetry of Mr. Housman strikes us at once by what it is not. Adrian Ross is the admitted successor to W. S. Gilbert, and Hilaire Belloc to Edward Lear; while Owen Seaman, G. E. Farrow, and many others have divided the mantle of the Rev. Charles Dodgson. Mr. Housman must be counted one of the few whose note in fantasy is wholly his own. Lord Alfred Douglas is of the company. Nobody else could possibly have written 'Dear me! The Bee.' Mr. Anstey Guthrie enjoys the extraordinary privilege of being most wholly distinct and himself when professedly imitating or parodying another. But it would be difficult to name a fourth. Here are some lines taken at hazard from Mr. Housman :—

'We combed out the miles with invincible feet.'
(*Gods and their Makers*, p. 44.)

'Flower of night, flower of night,
Come and stand within the light,
And look into the heavens above
Where the moon hangs like a hive,
And the stars are all alive,
For the stars are the bees of love.'
(*Prunella*, p. 48.)

A Mercian of the Welsh marches, Mr. Housman has brought with him from that old England that was by the Baltic a singularly vivid recollection of the weirdness and savagery of the old North. He is reverent in Zion, but terribly at home in a world that knew such troubling of its waters as are indicated in *The Dome*, such horrors of the snowy waste as are illustrated in *The Werewolf*. The book which bears this latter title is by the author's sister, Miss Clemence Housman; it was published as early as 1896 in London and, rather oddly, in Chicago. The illustrations, by Mr. Housman, are already counted among the treasures of those who collect his 'early period.' The very beautiful and simply designed cover is by him, but neither that nor the lovely initial T, in the Byzantine manner, are consonant with the elemental and brutal note of the main theme. The great thing, of course, from the artist's point of view, is to arrive. Expression is the object. The picture on p. 12, where the small boy is hugging the big lad's feet, might have appeared in the famous *Tennyson* of 1857. But it is absolutely non-derivative; only the lighting in some ways suggests Arthur Hughes. 'The Race' (p. 84) is magnificent; the hurrying gait of White Fell and the long stride of the Avenger are telling the story for us as we gaze. There is in this splendid drawing something that Aubrey Beardsley never quite reached with the pencil; though Count Eric Stenbock in England and Guy de Maupassant in France (so also Apuleius in his decadent Latin) have reached it in prose. The 'Dead Wolf' in the illustration to p. 121 is not efficient, but the two figures are very beautifully expressed, and the distinction between life and death is finely indicated in every line. From this powerful work, yet of an early period, we may appropriately step back to the illustrations of *Weird Tales from Northern Seas,* which was published in 1893, and contains quite boyish designs, in which we see none the less the strength coming. This volume, which was a dead failure, and was disposed of as a 'remainder' by the author, Mr. Nisbet Bain, at the most modest prices of the Charing Cross Road, is extraordinarily repulsive, and will undoubtedly be worth collecting. Mr. Bain has translated with absolute fidelity from a Norwegian folk-lorist, who himself set down the tales of the more primitive Norwegians in their crudest form. The *Volsunga Saga,* which dates from the times of Hengist and Horsa, is moderate, almost modern by the side of these narrations in which human beings and theriomorphs no longer contrast, because the human being in his normal state is still a beast of the field and wood. The story of the *Gan* Finn (compare the *Ganic* flies of the Kálevalá) in the hands of even the earliest Greeks would have taken on a sympathetic touch, but SEIMKÉ, the heroine, is unmaidenly at the first, repellent at the last, and the artist with true insight has illustrated not p. 27, where the girl does not wait to be loved, or p. 59 where the escape begins, but p. 26 with the uncanny *Gan* Finn, who is *the* interesting figure to the primitive Norwegian. Dante did not traverse the *Inferno* unscathed, and Mr. Housman has not wholly escaped contamination from the abominable regions explored by Mr. Bain. It is a relief to know that Swift never was in a position to write of primitive Norway, and that Beardsley was never in a position to illustrate his writing.

In *Gods and their Makers* (John Lane, 1897) we have an early fantasy. 'Glory to Man in the Highest' appears to be its message, especially in such passages as that of pp. 125-28, where the gods compete for Peeti's worship and he finds himself commanding them unawares. The unloosing of Champurn is quite Hesiodic, a piece of an old Theogony with its Titanomachia to hold the attention of a fighting people. In the end we find God to be the birth of a vain supplication; from man the master of It (p. 213). The mood in which this book was written is peculiar. It is Ernest Haeckel writing a fairy tale. We

shall not find it in Mr. Housman's later or more characteristic works, neither is it his essential note. We wonder what unanswered prayers of 1896 had led to this sublimer petulance of a believing man. Coming to recent work, *The Cloak of Friendship* (London: Murray, 1905), we have a broad, wise, and cheerful outlook in what we imagine to be the later stories, but there is an intense sense of the power of evil in those that we can identify as collected from earlier sources. There is great beauty, and a synthesis of reconciliation, in the verses dedicatory :—

1. 'O moving friends, that unrevealed,
      Through dusk or dark or break of day,
   Bring seed to bless the common field
      Where the worn ploughshare lifts the clay.

2. Ye, that stand shadows of a light
      More fair than man has not to see,
   Come from your homes of day or night
      And lay the covering Cloak on me :

3. And in that shelter let me share
      The gifts of time which yet remain,
   Ye that gave warmth and light and air
      And sought no recompense again.

4. So shall the friends I have not wronged
      Take root within my life and grow—
   This dust of life where once belonged
      The hearts I sought to know.'

We pass to a volume of poems which made a deep impression :—

   '"This unguent, boy, is truly excellent."
   '"Of course it is ; 'tis Spikenard." '

So Menander in his *Cecryphalus,* and many will be inclined to agree with him in perusing the *Spikenard* (London, 1898) of Mr. Housman. No living poet has bettered the Annunciation Song (p. 7):—

1. 'A garden bower in bower
      Grew waiting for God's hour :
   Where no man ever trod,
      This was the gate of God.

2. The first bower was red ;
      Her lips which "welcome" said.
   The second bower was blue ;
      Her eyes that let God through.

3. The third bower was white ;
      Her soul in God's sight.
   Three bowers of love
      Won Christ from Heaven above.'

The Work of Laurence Housman 231

Reverting to prose—for our author's production has changed its medium indifferently, using always that best for his current theme—in the 'Defence of Farringdon' (*The Dome*, 1st Jan. 1899), where 'sleep was torn up by the roots,' we have an unusual stateliness of beautiful and considered diction, differing much from the intentional violence of much in *Antæus*, though *Antæus* is not quite two years later. Johnson would never have done more than curb this incurable romantic; Meredith exaggerates where he influences, and we sometimes topple over into the bizarre. 'The asperities of poverty have separated her from the locality of her romance; and it is the dream of a day yet to come, in which she sees herself revisiting the place whose honour her pride indeed saved, yet, as the Scripture says, "so, as by fire."' This is the ending of the 'Defence of Farringdon,' into which the author has put much strength and no violence. Both strength and violence are the notes of a very early story (*The Dome*, 24th June 1897), interesting because the author has supplied a whole page illustration by way of frontispiece to the tale itself, and because the illustration might pass with the most observant for a woodblock of the best period of the 'sixties.' In its nervous strength and passion it recalls Sandys, the fallen figure is intentionally misshapen, and the whole is marked rather by the mood in which the Signy stories were written in the *Volsunga Saga* than by any contemporary pen. *The Troubling of the Waters* is not agreeable reading, but it would have interested Balzac and, one imagines, Ibsen. It is quite Northern and rather altruistic than decadent. It is well, perhaps, that it should remain unique of its kind.

Antæus (London: Murray, 1901) is thoroughly mature work. There is a strong, simple story to tell, and it is well told. The writer holds on unfalteringly to his course, and while in an early chapter—on his third page, indeed—he points out how modern we indeed are even when we ape the classical, he is in truth more classical in his conception of this particular tale than we find him elsewhere. He does not turn aside to the right or the left any more than does Mr. Meredith in his *Egoist*. The book of Mr. Housman ends in the failing and passing of Antæus as the book of

Mr. Meredith ends in Sir Willoughby Patterne's humiliation. But in either case the end was *voulu* from the first. The sexual element in *Antæus* is healthily handled, and there is no unpleasant taste left in the mouth, but the reader all the same is not pleased. Mr. Housman here writes with at once the restraint and the knowledge of a man. If *An Englishwoman's Love Letters* is a *tour de force* in insight into a feminine attitude, the book which followed it says in every chapter that it could only have been written by a man. Why, then, has the reader a quarrel with *Antæus*? The answer is clear enough. Nobody likes to be reminded that the healthy and normal advent of sex glamour clouds the intellect and perverts the will. Love itself is but a rosy mist which rises between the Seer and the Seen. The great creation of *Antæus*, however, is Lady Petwyn, a living personage added to the very limited list of realities in fiction.

Sabrina Warham (London: Murray, 1904) is a novel of exceptional power, distinguished by a good and well-developed plot, and marked by the firm delineation of some living and notable characters. It is Thomas Hardy's country that is the scene of the story, but the manner is quite distinct. The old farmer, Lady Derrers, and the hero, David, appeal to us more than Sabrina herself. But we like her best, and then very well, on the last page where she says 'There is home' and David answers 'Ay, I reckon it 'll be home now.'

Prunella, the play which alone thus far of Mr. Housman's works has received the approbation of the Censor, has a sensuous, almost a sensual, note, which is not to be found in the prohibited *Bethlehem*. The old story of the ideal gone wrong is very charmingly presented, but we are surprised at the *finale*, which is serious poetry of a high order—

'Hush, hush, the birds are waking in the night,
They sing of thee and me and our delight.

. . . . . .

'Tis not the birds: it is the stars that sing;
Nay, not the stars, nor any mortal thing
Either in earth beneath or heaven above;
The song thou hearest is the song of Love!'

And to the notes of Love's viol there comes the dawning of the perfect Day.

The *Vicar of Wakefield*, produced at the Prince

of Wales's, was so much altered by the manager, Mr. Curzon, that Mr. Housman had no alternative but to disown the work. The alterations were such as, in the opinion of the writer, not only to rob the play of artistic value, but to constitute a vital perversion of the original masterpiece of Goldsmith. To this no self-respecting man of letters could lend himself. The object of the changes was the usual one, that of giving a certain actress the best things, not of her own part, but of other characters. With the plays may be mentioned *The Venture*, an annual for which, in 1903, Mr. Housman was in part responsible. It is a handsome quarto and bears on its covers a vigorous drawing : a terminal or caryatid figure of Love the Archer. The type is extremely manly and the drawing shows a strong line. *The Proverbial Romances*, nine in number, are an interesting essay in a form which lies midway between folklore and fiction.

The Little Land (London : Richards, 1899) and *Green Arras* (London : Lane, 1896) contain some of the author's finest and most characteristic verse. We have already spoken of the former ; in the latter we have

'The loves and the lives of whose grieving
I strove to make music and day,'

as the poet tells us. There is a 'Song of the Road' (p. 1) full of that feeling for the open country which never deserts us in Mr. Housman's company ; there is 'Antæus' (p. 9), which in part forecast the novel and has a noble illustration ; there is 'Buried Treasure' (p. 54), where we surely feel again the mystic peace and rapt beauty that are so marvellous in Rossetti's 'Staff and Scrip.' William Morris has influenced the writer of 'The Dead Comrade' (p. 70), but this is nearer to the real thing than the wealthy Socialist ever got. It is not so beautiful as Morris at his best, but it has the *allure* of a thing where the theme lifts the author along and ends by speaking itself. 'The Great Ride' (p. 84) is Buddhist in conception, and utters with a very reasonable energy the contempt that so many lovers of animals feel for a mere Saviour of men. The essential brotherhood and comradeship of all life is as Aryan as the 'for thy pleasure they are and were created' is Semitic.

A Tale of a Nun (Philadelphia, 1901, privately printed) is from a story of the year 1320 preserved in the very difficult *patois* of Flanders in that early period. Mr. L. Simons having Englished it literally, a task of no little care, Mr. Housman has put it into that graceful and melodious literary English that we appreciate in *Amoris and Amabel*. The note is of a sincere Catholic piety. 'And we all of us that hear or read, let us pray Mary may be our advocate in this sweet valley where God shall sit and doom the world. Amen.'

'The New Orpheus' (*The Dome*, 1st Feb. 1899) is a very characteristic poem, the theme being St. Francis of Assisi and the communion of the animal world with humanity, the mystery to which the great saint of Italy is regarded as having the clue. The stanza on the Living Creatures in the Apocalypse is remarkable for its firm hold on legends, or shall we say doctrines, that to the modern mind are strangely vague.

Mr. Housman's writings as a controversialist on the Church side are buried in the columns of an anonymous press, but some have not ceased laughing over a club impromptu when the Archbishop of Canterbury declared the invocation of saints to be contrary to the doctrines of the Church of England :—

1. 'Faith of our Fathers, what a smirch
You wear upon your dumb front !
Now that the law-established Church
Denies the Church Triumphant.

2. Religious truth, like household jam,
In measured jars she jambeth ;
Behold the Canterbury Lamb :
Its freezing depôt, Lambeth !'

This is not the only epigram which has been launched from a ready bow. Mr. Housman's contributions to the *Manchester Guardian* being for the most part signed are better known to the world of readers. They deal with leading art exhibitions, and occasionally with some leading book on art. Much thought and many felicities of expression are buried in these articles, and it may be hoped that the author will one day find time to rally these 'lost leaders' to the banner of a Book of Essays on Art and Artists. But Mr. Housman is a busy man.

All Fellows (London : Kegan Paul, 1896) has something of the *chant fable* about it, but the stories are separate gems to which the verse

The Work of Laurence Housman

supplies a chain. The method, therefore, is in reality more akin to Rossetti's ' Rosemary ' and to Tennyson's ' Princess,' though in both these cases, of course, lyric verse was the link connecting narrative poetry, not prose.

The note of epicurean æstheticism is very strong in *All Fellows*, and especially in the drawings. These are exceedingly beautiful, intense in feeling, lovely in design. 'The Truce of God' (p. 21) is extraordinarily graceful, and the opulence of pleasure which it affords in the studying supplies the real contrast to the emaciation of the figures. There is deliberate exaggeration of length in the body of the beautiful kneeling youth in ' The Merciful Drought' (p. 59), in that of the figure at the spring (frontispiece to *The Little Land*), perhaps in that on p. 53 of *The Sensitive Plant*, but in this last case an immense sense of uplifting motion is obtained, and the fine line-work of this singularly beautiful etching is itself thoroughly in sympathy (do not methods and even processes have sympathies?) with their etiolation, which is not hebetude but an image of the spirit's importance in comparison with the body.

Pen-work is extremely akin to Mr. Housman's most intimate genius, its infinite delicacies are within his control and interpretive power more than are those of the poetic word itself. If compelled to say whether the artist or the writer had the most of this man's heart, one would be decided, I think, by his pen-work to say the artist, because the great majority of us when seeking to express the extremely delicate explore the felicity of words, which are akin to the sense sound. Mr. Housman explores the felicity of line, which is akin to the sense of touch. It is the difference between the song and the kiss, and as ' B. V.' has told us, lovers' lips only express the former when they cannot impress the latter. In his finest things in thin pen-line Mr. Housman is at least as great as Millais, he is nearer to Rossetti in feeling, while possessing the advantage of being able to draw and suggest the figure in three dimensions instead of two. The extremely beautiful study of a Lady and Tortoise, which we are privileged to give from an original drawing by the artist, will tell the reader more at a glance than much writing could enforce. Work like this not only proclaims itself as of the

first class in all that makes for beauty of thought and execution, but while clearly belonging to a school is derived directly from the fount of inspiration on which the whole school drew. The *Amigo di Botticelli* is not a copyist of Botticelli; Mr. Housman in this exquisite drawing is not a copyist of Rossetti and Millais. But the period of either can be dated quite surely; the *Amigo* is not earlier than the influences which whisper to us from the *tondi* of Filipepi, nor is Mr. Housman's lady in this study earlier than the Ophelia of Millais, the Blessed Damozel of Rossetti, and the ' Beautiful Lady' (this a poetic conception purely, never reduced to picture) of Woolner.

'Give the Devil his Due,' which has the dreamy glamour of silverpoint about its pencil-work, is suggestive of a Kate Greenaway period, but the goat-footed deity is a wholly original presentation of an old conception. This is a drawing that will probably be collected; it has great beauties, and is a synthesis of more than one movement.

The 'Well in the Wall' (*The Dome*, 29th Sept. 1897) is an exquisite piece of architectural drawing, the arches supplying a wonderful series of harmonising and contrasting curves. The figures are put in with care, but are not hard as in the vast majority of architectural drawings. That of the more distant figures is rather small for the distance to be indicated, but the effect of space is greatly increased; we cannot with this *raffiné* be sure that the error was not intentional.

The female figure in Mr. Housman's drawings is perhaps less prominent than the male, but there are very interesting evidences of a wide range of interest. Now and again, as in the frontispiece to *Prunella* (London : Bullen, 1906), the type takes us back to the early Victorian era, and we are surprised that Prunella herself is to be taken so. The Pierrot and the Scaramel are of the late seventeenth century. The frontispiece to *All Fellows* is a very graceful study of the female nude. The figures in the distance are admirably in motion, while that to the right in the foreground is in the very act of disrobing. There is an absolute absence of woodenness from Mr. Housman's drawing, which divides him by a great gulf from the neo-mediævalists. Nature in his pictures is often at repose, humanity never, so that the latter has no time to become ligneous as in the carved oak figures of Madox Brown's 'Labour' and of Holman Hunt's 'Shadow of the Cross.' As long ago as 1896 it was noted by the then art critic of the *Manchester Guardian* that in some of Mr. Housman's drawings the heads of some of the figures were 'preposterously small,' but we have only found this observation of R. A. M. Stevenson correct with respect to early work, and especially is it limited to the female figure. It is to be noted that the error inclines to the Greek and not to the mediæval. But in some of Mr. Housman's best early work it is wholly absent. Note the exquisite drawing of 'The Corn-Keeper,' one of the most beautiful drawings (landscape, with woman and child) that the last decade of the nineteenth century produced from any hand. Here there is veritable enchantment in flowing curves and waving corn. A different idea of the Female Figure is presented in the magistral drawing of 'Night,' the sceptred, cloaked, observant Queen, which forms, by the artist's kind permission, the frontispiece to this article. Strength and sweetness, the Woman Regnant, this seated figure lingers in the memory and connects the artist's work in spirit with the great sculptors in low relief who gave us the Nereid monument and the Drum of Ephesus and the many *stêlai* commemorative of maidens gone too soon to Corê, of well-loved *Ephêbi*, to the underworld. Of a different type naturally are the illustrations to *Jump to Glory Jane*, by George Meredith (London: Swan Sonnenschein, 1892), but these realise the lean figure, long face, wistful eyes, touching exaltation and 'blood at the spin with activity' which Meredith desiderated. They do not provoke a mocking smile, but excite a curious interest combined with a strong sense of the mystic :—

'May those who ply the tongue that cheats,
And those who rush to beer and meats,
And those whose mean ambition aims
At palaces and titled names,
Depart in such a cheerful strain
As did our Jump to Glory Jane.'

Meredith feels it and the artist feels it. The figure in the last picture is very beautiful, and all that Meredith had to say. The attendant figures are hardly adequate.

Writing of Blake, a somewhat kindred subject to the Celtic *ecstatica*, Mr. Housman has assigned to him 'the thoughtlessness and glory of a flower' (*Blake's Works*, ed. Laurence Housman. London: Kegan Paul, 1893). Our critic has not noticed Blake's very deliberate reversion to a Turanian formalism, a *chinoiserie*. Blake claimed to have made the number of syllables a set study in a piece, just as to this day the Japanese 'strict forms' go by syllables, twenty-one in one form, thirty-one in another, usually five in a line, with an extra syllable to give that effect which in *rubaiyàt* is given by the unrhymed line. Mr. Housman quotes with approval Blake's admirable *aperçu*, 'The face and limbs that deviate or alter least from infancy to old age are the face and limbs of greatest beauty and perfection.'

A poem which Mr. Housman was thoroughly in sympathy with when illustrating, is Shelley's *Sensitive Plant* (London, 1898). In this volume perhaps his finest line-work will be found. The illustration facing the twentieth page is beyond what any of the great illustrators of the Victorian era from 1850 to 1870 achieved. It has the precision and the decision, the design and the detail of the great Pre-Raphaelites, but is free from their invincible quaintness, and Rossetti as we know felt that to be their fault, and hated the man who called his drawings 'quaint.' The face has the haunting beauty of a drawing by Gustave Moreau, and it has soul besides.

We may note, when studying our artist's designs, the influence of Houghton in 'the Tree of Guile' (*All Fellows*, p. 75), of Cruikshank (possibly) in the frontispiece to *Prunella*, of Charles Ricketts in the *Goblin Market* (but not elsewhere), of Beardsley in the front page of *Elfintown* (but not elsewhere). The influences are as they should be there, and they are, as they should be, all early. In *Elfintown*, a poem by Jane Harlow (London: Macmillan, 1894), most of Mr. Housman's drawings are of interest. It was a people of very bushy hair that built Elfintown, but the drawing of the nearest figure on p. 21 is beautiful, and the watching Queen is particularly well designed. The 'Term' (p. 25) is 'quite Housman,' not Hellenic but absolutely non-Pre-Raphaelite. The artist is already coming into his kingdom in which we

The Work of Laurence Housman

shall soon come to know him as unquestioned master even as we know a Burne-Jones, a Fred Walker, a Linley Sambourne, a Sime. There is always something of greatness about this separateness. It is said in the word Distinction. Yet of course some very great artists can hardly be said to have it : there are Raven Hills that bridge the remoteness of Charles Keene, drawings by W. Small that press on Tenniel. The Faun-eared figure under the Dandelions (p. 29) should be studied for its 'strangeness in beauty.' The same year, 1894, gave us *A Farm in Fairyland* (London : Kegan Paul), where Mr. Housman has a theme wholly suitable to a lover of both farms and fairies. He is here, too, his own illustrator, though it should very particularly be noted that he is one of the most fortunate of artists in interpreting the literature and poetry of others. Certainly he has more sympathy than the vast majority of men who set themselves to another's theme. One word before we leave this volume. There is a cat in it (p. 98) which would delight Caran d'Ache.

Mr. Housman is strangely at home in fairyland. There is, in fact, something distinctly uncanny about this obvious and serious familiarity with a place that is not a place ' within the meaning of the Act.' What makes this circumstance the more suspicious is the want of evidence of any development in the knowledge. He always seems to have had it. He was writing with critical judgment of 'A Capful of Moonshine' (*The Dome*, 1st Oct. 1898) at a quite early date, and this story is exceedingly finished work, a minor 'Père Goriot,' *à rebours*. In his preface to

Gammer Grethel's Fairy Tales (London : Moring, 1905) he writes : 'The true end and object of a fairy tale is the expression of the joy of living. There begins and ends the morality of the fairy tale : its value consists in its optimism. So for the true and unpolluted air of fairyland we have to go back to the old and artless tales of a day purer and simpler than our own ; purer because so wholly unconcerned with any question of morals, simpler because so wholly unconscious of its simplicity.' This is well said, and is, if one mistakes not, a clue to Mr. Housman himself. This is why we feel that his is not the morrow of Epicurean asceticism, but the after-morrow of Catholicism. The agnostic will go to church to escape the suspicion of Mackennaïsm, he will remain to appreciate, and appreciating will end in praise. Mr. Housman meanwhile will have arrived at the same goal by way of this same fairyland where morals are never dwelt on, and so the clue to religion is never lost. It will not be the embroidered copes which will attract him, as the millinery and satin slippers were thought by Ruskin to attract the modern child to the modern Märchen. But it will be the Mystery which the cope is worn to honour, even as the children of pre-Reformation England were chiefly attracted, as again says the Sage of Coniston, by the enchantments that the fairies worked. And if anything in the future will entice the really wise to leave the authentic garden of Epicurus (which is the garden of unexhausting pleasures, the pleasures of the soul), that temptation will be Mr. Housman's, luring the world to Old Religion by way of a walk through Fairyland.

[NOTE.—The two illustrations and the initial letter are from original drawings by Mr. Housman, and are here reproduced for the first time by kind permission of the artist.]

Tailpiece from Goblin Market, *1893.*

NOTES

Chapter I

1 Laurence Housman, 'Pre-Raphaelitism in Art and Poetry', in *Essays by Divers Hands*, 1933, p.29.
2 Laurence Housman, *The Unexpected Years*, 1937, pp.7-8. Hereafter referred to as 'UY'.
3 John Pugh, *Bromsgrove and the Housmans*, 1974, p.lxii.
4 UY, p.13.
5 UY, pp. 26-30.
6 UY, p.35.
7 Quoted by Richard Perceval Graves in *A.E.Housman, The Scholar Poet*, 1981 edition, p.13.
8 *Ibid.*, p.21.
9 Quoted by Maude Hawkins in *A.E.Housman: Man behind a Mask*, 1958, p.40.
10 *Dictionary of National Biography*, entry written by Roger Fulford.
11 Graves, p.27.
12 UY, p.19.
13 UY, p.62.
14 UY, p.103.
15 See item 250 in National Book League catalogue, *The Housmans*, 1975.
16 Pugh, p.xxxv.
17 UY, p.105.
18 UY, p.20.
19 UY, p.102.
20 UY, p.93.

Chapter II

1 Laurence Housman to Maude Hawkins, 29 May 1958, Library of Congress.
2 Graves, p.64.
3 Published in *The Cornhill*, July, 1895.
4 UY, p.105.
5 The critic was Mabel Cox in *The Artist*, 1898. p.99; see critic chapter.
6 UY, p.108.
7 UY, pp.108-109

8 See Street Library, Housman collection catalogue, 1967, item 16.
9 See National Book League, *The Housmans*, item 249.
10 *The Studio*, 1896, p.224.
11 UY, pp.124-125.
12 Laurence Housman, 'National Art Training', Manchester Municipal School of Art, 18 September 1911.
13 UY, p.107; R.L.Green, *Andrew Lang*, 1946, *passim*.
14 UY, p.109.

Chapter III

1 Quoted by Derek Hudson, *Arthur Rackham*, 1974 reprint, p.32.
2 I.K.Hodgkins, *Laurence Housman*, 1978, item 504.
3 UY, p.111.
4 Holbrook Jackson, *The Eighteen Nineties*, 1976 reprint, p.30.
5 UY, p.113.
6 See Hodgkins, item 578.
7 Graves, p.268; UY, p.138.
8 UY, p.146.
9 Roger Fulford in DNB.
10 UY, p.112.
11 *Universal Review*, 1890, pp.209, 222.
12 Preface to *Jump to Glory Jane*, 1892, pp.26-27.
13 UY, pp.116-117.
14 Sir Geoffrey Keynes, *Complete Writings of William Blake*, 1957, p.611.
15 J.Lewis May, *John Lane and the Nineties*, 1936, p.45.
16 UY, pp.113, 115.
17 John Russell Taylor, *The Art Nouveau Book in Britain*, 1966, pp.108-109.
18 Laurence Housman to John Lane, 30 August, 1 September 1893, Huntington Library.
19 Housman to Lane, 6 September 1893, Huntington Library.
20 *The Studio*, November 1893, p.58.

21 Housman to Lane, 9 September 1893, Huntington Library.

22 Housman to Lane, letters dated 20, 28 September, 11 October and (? December) 1893, Huntington Library.

23 James G.Nelson, *The Early Nineties,* 1971, p.64.

24 UY, pp.118-119; *Colby Library Quarterly,* June 1973, pp.116, 113.

25 Katherine Lyon Mix, *A Study in Yellow,* 1960, p.40.

26 Lewis May, p.184; UY, p.111.

27 Housman to Lane, 4 October and n.d. (Alnwick) 1893, Huntington Library.

28 Laurence Housman, *Arthur Boyd Houghton,* 1896, p.22. Hereafter as 'ABH'.

29 Brian North Lee, *British Book-plates,* 1976, p.98.

30 *Modern Book-plates and their Designers, The Studio,* Special Number, Winter 1898-1899, p.20.

31 Housman, ABH, p.11.

32 Housman, ABH, p.18.

33 Charles Kains-Jackson in *The Book-Lovers Magazine,* 1908, p.230.

34 Housman to Lane, 10 December 1893, Huntington Library.

35 Quoted in Simon Nowell-Smith, *Letters to Macmillan,* 1963, p.238.

36 *Ibid.,* p.239.

37 R.E.D.Sketchley, *English Book Illustration of Today,* 1903, p.16.

38 Leonée and Richard Ormond, *Lord Leighton,* 1975, pp.117-118; UY, p.118.

39 Housman to Lane, 9, 16 January 1894, Huntington Library.

40 Holbrook Jackson, p.46.

41 Housman to Lane, 20 April 1894, Huntington Library.

42 Lewis May, pp.68-69.

Chapter IV

1 UY, pp.101, 103.

2 See Anne Born, 'Clemence Housman's First Book', *Housman Society Journal,* 1977, pp.57-66.

3 Housman's own obituary, *Manchester Guardian,* 21 February 1959.

4 Kains-Jackson, p.235.

5 Housman's preface to *Gammer Grethel's Fairy Tales,* 1905.

6 Kains-Jackson, p.235.

7 Laurence Housman in *The Bibliophile,* July 1908, pp.232-233.

8 *Magazine of Art,* March 1899, pp.199-205.

9 UY, pp.161-162.

Chapter V

1 Laurence Housman, *My Brother: AEH,* 1937, p.75. Hereafter referred to as 'AEH'.

2 *The Times,* 21 February 1959.

3 Kains-Jackson, p.234.

4 *The Athenaeum,* 9 January 1897, p.42.

5 UY, pp.118, 127-128.

6 Hodgkins, p.2.

7 Street catalogue, p.1.

8 Rupert Hart-Davis, *Letters of Oscar Wilde,* 1962, p.713.

9 Graves, pp.130-131.

10 Kains-Jackson, p.233.

11 Sketchley, p.17.

12 *Magazine of Fine Arts,* November 1905, p.15.

13 *Ibid.,* p.83; 1906, pp.406ff.

14 *The Bibliophile,* July 1908, p.232.

15 William E.Fredeman, *Pre-Raphaelitism,* 1965, pp.29-30.

16 UY, pp.152-157.

Chapter VI

1 *The Studio,* Special Number, Winter 1899-1900, p.20.

2 *Colby Library Quarterly,* June 1973, p.117.

3 Kains-Jackson, p.231.

4 *Print Collector's Quarterly,* 1924, pp.190-204.

5 See Taylor, pp.111-112. For an illustrated list of Woodroffe's work see Peter Cormack, *Paul Woodroffe,* 1982 (William Morris Gallery, Walthamstow).

Chapter VII

1 Max Beerbohm, *Seven Men,* 1966 edition, p.5.

2 UY, pp.126-127.

3 See *The Studio,* 15 May 1904, pp.301-312, for Housman on Herbert's work.

4 Holbrook Jackson, p.89.

5 Hart-Davis, p.771; original in Street Library.

6 Laurence Housman, *Echo de Paris,* 1923, p.26.

7 William Gaunt, *Aesthetic Adventure,* 1945, p.171.

8 Laurence Housman to Henry Davray, 8 January 1901, Huntington Library.

9 Robert Ross, *Friend of Friends,* 1952, p.89. The caricatures are in the Street Library collection.

10 Housman to Henry Davray, 7 January 1902, Huntington Library.

11 Ross, p.90.

12 AEH, p.104.

13 Quoted by Anne Born, *Housman Society Journal,* 1977, p.57.

14 Ross, pp.91-92.

15 Housman to H.de V.Stacpoole, 13 July 1904, British Library.

16 *Somerset Evening World,* 20 February 1959.

17 *The Times,* 21 February 1959.

Chapter VIII

1 Denys Sutton, *Letters of Roger Fry,* 1972, Volume I, p.334.

2 *The Studio,* 1898, p.252.

3 UY, p.120.

4 UY, p.9.

5 *Letters of George Meredith,* 1970, Volume II, p.1379.

6 See Katherine Lyon Mix, 'An Englishwoman's Love-Letters', in the *Housman Society Journal,* 1977, pp.28-37.

7 UY, p.114.

8 Diana L.Johnson in *Fantastic Illustration and Design in Britain, 1850-1930,* Rhode Island School of Design, 1979, p.71.

9 AEH, p.163.

10 *The Studio,* Special Number, 1897-1898, p.58.

11 Ross, p.169.

12 For a sales record of Lane's books in America see Nelson, pp.306-312.

13 I.K.Hodgkins, *passim.*

APPENDICES

<hr>

A

BOOKS DESIGNED AND ILLUSTRATED BY LAURENCE HOUSMAN

Note: The following list includes works written by Housman and others, compiled from Ian Kenyur Hodgkins, Laurence Housman Collection, 1978, the British Library catalogue, and private collections. Arranged chronologically, descriptions are for first editions.

1888
The Elect Lady by George Macdonald
London: Kegan Paul, Trench, Trübner & Co.
Housman's earliest published design used as frontispiece.

1892
Jump to Glory Jane by George Meredith, edited and arranged by Harry Quilter
London: Swan, Sonnenschein & Co.
"With forty-four Designs Invented, Drawn and Written by Laurence Housman", which included frontispiece, seven full-page illustrations and thirty-six text inserts, the text hand-written by Housman, process engraved. 1,000 copies printed, 250 ordered for America by Macmillan & Co. Limited edition bound in vellum, with gold blocked cover, 100 copies.

1892
Preferences in Art, Life, and Literature by Harry Quilter
London: Swan, Sonnenschein & Co.
Cover design (gilt on blue cloth) and title-page by Housman. Large paper edition in full vellum gilt with new cover design is also known.

1893
Book-Plates by W.J. Hardy
London: Kegan Paul, Trench, Trübner & Co.
Decorative half-title by Housman, re-used for all works in the series 'Books about Books', edited by A.W. Pollard.

1893
Goblin Market by Christina Rossetti
London: Macmillan & Co.
Cover design (gilt on green cloth), beige dust-wrappers printed in green repeating the cover design, half-title vignette, pictorial title, thirty-three text illustrations and decorations, four full-page and four double-page illustrations. Coloured copy by Gloria Cardew of the Guild of Women Binders; large paper copy of 160 copies; reissue Macmillan, 1909, with illustrations reduced and printed in brown, new borders to title and frontispiece.

1893
Poems by Francis Thompson
London: Elkin Mathews & John Lane; Boston: Copeland & Day
Grey paper boards with cover design, orange-printed title and frontispiece by Housman. First edition 500 copies; second impression 500 copies; seventh edition 500 copies in pale green cloth gilt.

1893
Weird Tales from Northern Seas by R. Nisbet Bain, from the Danish of Jonas Lie
London: Kegan Paul, Trench, Trübner & Co.
Twelve full-page illustrations by Housman, blue cloth binding blocked in gold.

1894
The End of Elfin-Town by Jane Barlow
London: Macmillan & Co.
Cover design in light brown cloth gilt, dust-wrapper beige and ochre design, pictorial title, six large text illustrations and eight full-page drawings by Housman. Large paper edition of 50 copies also known.

1894
A Farm in Fairyland by Laurence Housman
London: Kegan Paul, Trench, Trübner & Co.
Cover design (gilt on green cloth), pictorial title, initial letters and twelve full-page drawings to twelve fairy-tales. Large paper edition limited to 50 copies with full-page illustrations on Japanese vellum.

1894
A Random Itinerary by John Davidson
London: Elkin Mathews & John Lane; Boston: Copeland & Day
Cover design (gilt on pink cloth), orange-printed title and frontispiece by Housman. First edition of 600 copies.

1894
Cuckoo Songs by Katharine Tynan Hinkson
London: Elkin Mathews & John Lane; Boston: Copeland & Day
Cover design (pink cloth gilt), and pictorial title by Housman. First edition of 500 copies.

1895
The House of Joy by Laurence Housman
London: Kegan Paul, Trench, Trübner & Co.
Cover design (green cloth, upper cover design blocked in green and gold), pictorial title, initial letters and eight full-page illustrations to the eight fairy-tales. Second edition in darker cloth.

1895
Bibliographica. Papers on Books, their History and Art. Volume I
London: Kegan Paul, Trench, Trübner & Co.
Title page vignette in black by Housman.

1895
A Pomander of Verse by Edith Nesbit
London: John Lane at The Bodley Head; Chicago:
A.C.McClurg & Co.
Cover design (pink cloth gilt), pictorial title and one
ornament (repeated six times). First edition of 750
copies.

1895
The Viol of Love by Charles Newton-Robinson
London: John Lane at The Bodley Head; Boston:
Lamson, Wolffe & Co.
Cover design (green cloth gilt), title-page and four
designs in orange by Housman. First edition of 350
copies.

1895
Sister Songs. An Offering to Two Sisters by Francis
Thompson
London: John Lane at The Bodley Head; Boston:
Copeland & Day
Cover design (green cloth gilt), orange-printed title
and a frontispiece design by Housman.

1896
Green Arras by Laurence Housman
London: John Lane at The Bodley Head; Chicago:
Way & Williams
Cover design (green cloth gilt), yellow and white
decorated end-papers, frontispiece, pictorial title,
forty-three initials and five full-page illustrations.
First edition 850 copies.

1896
The Were-Wolf by Clemence Housman
London: John Lane at The Bodley Head; Chicago:
Way & Williams
Cover design (pink cloth gilt and blind-stamped),
orange-printed title and six full-page illustrations by
Housman, process engraved. First edition of 1000
copies; another edition bound in green with cover
design in blue.

1896
*All-Fellows. Seven Legends of Lower Redemption
with Insets in Verse* by Laurence Housman
London: Kegan Paul, Trench, Trübner & Co.
Cover design (green cloth gilt), title, initials and
seven illustrations to seven stories. Second edition
identical but for bright green cloth gilt.

1896
Dust in the Balance by George Knight
London: Jarrold & Sons
('Impressionist Series') Title-page design, repeated
on upper cover (green cloth gilt), by Housman.

1897
*The Flower of the Mind. A Choice among the best
Poems* edited by Alice Meynell
London: Grant Richards
Cover design (pale green cloth gilt) by Housman.

1898
The Field of Clover by Laurence Housman
London: Kegan Paul, Trench, Trübner & Co.
Cover design (bright green cloth, upper cover pictorially blocked in darker green and gold), initials, title,
frontispiece and ten full-page illustrations to ten
fairy-tales by Housman. Large paper copy known
with illustrations on Japanese vellum; small paper
edition (second impression) identical to first ordinary
edition except different cloth colour; American edition, New York: John Lane, 1902, in the bright green
cloth of first English edition.

1898
Selected Poems by George Meredith
London: Archibald Constable
Title-page vignette, incorporating the poet's initials,
by Housman. Later re-used in various Constable
editions of Meredith (see below).

1898
The Nature Poems of George Meredith
London: Archibald Constable & Co.
Title vignette by Housman, twenty photogravure
illustrations by William Hyde. Edition of 375 copies;
later edition with sixteen illustrations, without title
vignette but new binding design by Housman (blue
cloth gilt), 1907.

1898
Spikenard. A Book of Devotional Love-Poems by
Laurence Housman
London: Grant Richards; Boston: Richard G.Badger
& Co
Cover design (brown paper boards gilt) by Housman.
American edition identical except adverts omitted.

1898
The Sensitive Plant by Percy Bysshe Shelley
London: Aldine House
Cover design (blue cloth gilt), red and brown printed
title, initial letters and twelve full-page illustrations
by Housman. Special edition, one of ten copies for
the Guild of Women Binders, bound in dark blue
morocco, illustrations hand-coloured throughout by
Gloria Cardew, binding by Constance Karslake.
1899.

1899
The Little Land. With Songs from its Four Rivers
by Laurence Housman
London: Grant Richards
Cover design (grey boards gilt), frontispiece and
three full-page illustrations engraved by Clemence
Housman. Second edition with added imprint, Elkin
Mathews.

1899
The English Bookman's Library edited by Alfred
Pollard; *Volume I: English Embroidered Bookbind-
ings* by Cyril Davenport
London: Kegan Paul, Trench, Trübner & Co.
Title page border in black by Housman .

1899
The Silence of Love by Edmond Holmes
London and New York: John Lane
Cover design (blue cloth gilt), title and fifty initials
and tailpiece by Housman. Second edition printed
by the Birmingham Guild of Handicraft.

1899
On the Way Side. Verse and Translations by
C.Kegan Paul
London: Kegan Paul, Trench, Trübner & Co.
Floral border to title page designed by Housman.

1899
*Dante Gabriel Rossetti. An Illustrated Memorial of
his Art and Life* by H.C.Marillier
London: Bell & Sons
Cover design (blue cloth gilt) by Housman. Third
edition with cover reduced version of first edition,
1904.

1899
*Sweet Audrey. Scenes of Country Life and Town
Glamour* by George Morley

London: Jarrold & Sons
('Impressionist Series') Title vignette, repeated on upper cover, by Housman .

1899
Of the Imitation of Christ. In Four Books by Thomas A Kempis
Boston: L.C.Page & Co.; London: Kegan Paul, Trench, Trübner & Co.
Title border, frontispiece, initial letters, ornaments and three full-page illustrations by Housman, engraved by Clemence Housman. Edition of 660 copies on hand-made paper, bound in vellum gilt; also edition of 30 on Japanese vellum.

*   *   *

[1900]
At the Back of the North Wind by George Macdonald
London: Blackie & Sons, n.d.
Frontispiece and cover design (turquoise blue cloth blocked in dark blue and gold) by Housman, with seventy-five illustrations by Arthur Hughes. Later edition, cover design (red cloth, upper cover blocked in brown), on upper cover only, London & Glasgow: Blackie & Sons, n.d.

[1900]
The Princess and the Goblin by George Macdonald
London: Blackie & Sons, n.d.
Cover design uniform with the preceding volume, and frontispiece by Housman .

The above two volumes were part of a New Edition of Macdonald's 'Tales for Young People', published by Blackie from 1900 onwards. Other volumes in the series, issued with identical Housman cover, included:
The Princess and Curdie with illustrations by Helen Stratton
A Rough Shaking with illustrations by W.Parkinson
Ranald Bannerman's Boyhood with illustrations by Arthur Hughes
The History of Gutta Percha Willie with illustrations by Arthur Hughes .

*   *   *

1900
The Tale of Chloe by George Meredith
London: Archibald Constable & Co.
Title-page design by Housman (uniform edition with Selected Poems above).

1900
The Confessions of St. Augustine
London: Kegan Paul, Trench, Trübner & Co.
Title-page by Housman, illustrations by Paul Woodroffe, engraved by Clemence Housman.

1900
The Night by John White-Rodyng
London: Leonard Smithers
Frontispiece photogravure illustration by Housman to this collection of nine plays .

1902
Walt Whitman's Poetry. A Study and Selection by Edmond Holmes
London: John Lane at The Bodley Head
Cover design (green cloth blocked in dark green and gold) by Housman, uniform with *Silence of Love* above.

1902
Bethlehem. A Nativity Play performed with music by Joseph Moorat under the stage-direction of Edward Gordon Craig, December 1902
London: Macmillan & Co.
Cover design (grey paper boards, upper cover blocked in red) by Housman. First trade edition (green cloth gilt) cover design by Housman; reissued Macmillan, 1927; new edition Cape, 1955.

1903
The Triumph of Love by Edmond Holmes
London and New York: John Lane
Cover design (green cloth blocked in blue), uniform with *Silence of Love* and *Walt Whitman's Poetry* above, title design and sixty-three initials by Housman.

1904
The Blue Moon by Laurence Housman
London: John Murray
Cover design (blue cloth, upper cover pictorially blocked in blue and gold), pictorial title, frontispiece and eight full-page illustrations by Housman.

1905
The Cloak of Friendship by Laurence Housman
London: John Murray
Cover design (greenish brown cloth gilt) and seven initials to seven Housman stories.

1905
Maud by Alfred Tennyson
Campden, Gloucestershire: Essex House Press
Frontispiece design by Housman, drawn on wood block by Reginald Savage, engraved by Clemence Housman. Edition of 125 copies bound in white vellum, embossed rose on cover.

1906
Prunella, or Love in a Dutch Garden by Laurence Housman and H.Granville Barker
London: A.H.Bullen
Frontispiece design by Housman, bound in violet cloth. Later edition (beige cloth, upper cover blocked in red and blue with a 'sampler' design) by Housman, 1911; third edition, 1914; first American edition, Brentano's, 1906; later Boston: Little, Brown & Co., 1917.

[1908]
The Inner Way. Being Thirty-Six Sermons for Festivals by John Tauler
London: Methuen & Co., n.d.
Cover vignette, half-title and title-page border by Housman; re-used for 'Library of Devotion' series.

*   *   *

THE ST.FRANCIS PLAYS

1922
Little Plays of St.Francis. A Dramatic Cycle from the Life and Legend of St. Francis of Assisi by Laurence Housman, with preface by H.Granville Barker
London: Sidgwick & Jackson
Contains eighteen plays, each with a 'scene design' by Housman. Second edition 1923; fourth revised edition, 1926; sixth edition 1928; American edition (in mauve cloth) New York: Jonathan Cape and Harrison & Smith, [1926]. Also issued separately as Acting Editions, 1922-23, by Sidgwick & Jackson, with scene design on upper cover .

1923
Followers of St.Francis. Four Plays of the Early Franciscan Legend by Laurence Housman
London: Sidgwick & Jackson
Title vignette and four 'scene designs' by Housman. Published October 1923; second edition June 1925.

1926
The Comments of Juniper. Six Plays from the Life and Legend of St.Francis of Assisi by Laurence Housman
London: Sidgwick & Jackson
Title vignette and six 'scene designs' by Housman.

* * *

FAIRY-TALES AND STORIES COLLECTIONS

[1922]
A Doorway in Fairyland by Laurence Housman
London: Cape
Pictorial title-page, frontispiece and fourteen illustrations to twelve stories taken from the previous collections *A Farm in Fairyland, The House of Joy, The Field of Clover,* and *The Blue Moon.* American edition, New York: Harcourt Brace & Co., [1923] identical to English edition except for slate blue cloth binding (opposed to pinkish-grey cloth blocked in yellow and blue English binding); fourth impression, plain green cloth, title in blue upper cover and spine, [1937].

[1922]
Moonshine and Clover by Laurence Housman
London: Cape
Pictorial title, frontispiece and fourteen illustrations to this selection of eighteen stories from *A Farm in Fairyland, The House of Joy, The Field of Clover,* and *The Blue Moon.* American edition, New York: Harcourt Brace & Co., [1923] identical to English binding (slate-blue blocked in yellow and silver) except cloth is pinkish-grey, blocked in green and silver.

1923
All-Fellows and the Cloak of Friendship by Laurence Housman
London: Cape
Cover design (violet cloth, upper cover blocked in blue), cream dust-wrapper design, pictorial title and seven illustrations to fourteen stories from previous collections.

All-Fellows, the Cloak of Friendship
Another copy in pale grey-green cloth backed in dark green; American edition: Harcourt Brace & Co., n.d., slate-blue cloth blocked in green.

* * *

1925
The Death of Socrates. A Dramatic Scene founded upon two of Plato's Dialogues, the 'Crito' and the 'Phaedo', adapted for the stage by Laurence Housman
London: Sidgwick & Jackson
Title vignette by Housman, the book bound in red cloth with brick-red printed dust-wrappers.

B

MAGAZINES AND JOURNAL ILLUSTRATIONS BY LAURENCE HOUSMAN

The Apple of Beauty and Discord
Volume 1, No.1, First Quarter 1920
Contains three illustrations by Housman and "Wed-Away Hill", p.10.

Atalanta. The Victorian Magazine edited by L.T. Meade and A.B.Symington
Volume VI, No.61, October 1892
Contains 'The Corn Keeper', a Housman poem with two text illustrations and one full-page drawing, pp.57-59 (the full-page drawing, considerably altered in background and faces of figures, was published reduced size in *Green Arras,* 1896, op. p.35).
Volume VI, No.64, January 1893
Contains 'Royal Heart', a poem written and illustrated with two full-page drawings and three vignettes by Housman, pp.298-302.

The Beam edited by Alfred Jones
A Bi-Monthly Magazine published by some Art Students of the National Art Training School
No.3, May 1896
Contains 'A Study', a pen drawing by Housman, p.109.

The Bellman
1 July 1916
Contains three illustrations by Housman to 'The Death of St.Edmund', a poem by Walter W.Skeat. The drawings were made 1889-90 for *The Universal Review* (q.v.), but unpublished when the journal closed in 1890.

The Dome
London: The Unicorn Press
No.2, 24 June 1897
A Quarterly containing Examples of All the Arts. Contains story and frontispiece illustration, 'The Troubling of the Waters' by Housman, pp.27-47.
No.3, 29 September 1897
Contains the drawing, 'The Well in the Wall', p.11.
New Series, Volume 3, 1899
Contains the drawing, 'Cauchemar', p.123, printed on pure linen paper.

The Pageant edited by Gleeson White and C.H. Shannon
London: Henry & Co.
Volume 1, 1896
Contains 'Death and the Bather', a pen drawing by Housman, p.199.
Volume 2, 1897
Contains 'The Invisible Princess', a pen drawing to 'Blind Love' by Housman, p.125.

The Pall Mall Magazine
Volume 1, No.2, June 1893
Contains two pictorial borders and two headpieces to Rudyard Kipling's 'The Last Chanty', pp.129-32.
Volume 1, No.3, July 1893
Contains two illustrations by Housman to the Marchioness of Carmarthen's 'The Soul of Daphne', pp.284-94:

The Parade. An illustrated Gift Book for Boys and Girls
London: Henry & Co.
1897

Contains 'An Enchanted Princess' (i.e. 'The Bound Princess') with initials and one illustration, all by Housman, pp.64-93.

The Quarto. An Illustrated Annual
London: Virtue & Co.
Volume 4, 1898
Contains a drawing by Housman.

The Universal Review edited by Harry Quilter
Volume VII, July 1890
Contains Housman's story 'The Green Gaffer', illustrated with five full-page drawings and two ink insert drawings, pp.313-30; also George Barlow's 'The Singers of the Nineteenth Century', pp.503-20, with three full-page chalk drawings, two half-page, an initial 'W', and tailpiece, all by Housman.
Volume VIII, November 1890
Contains Richard Garnett's 'The Wisdom of the Indians', pp.366-72, with three full-page chalk drawings, initial 'E' and tailpiece by Housman.
Volume VIII, December 1890
Contains 'The Corn Witch', pp.539-41, with two full-page illustrations and vignette by Housman. (see also *The Bellman* entry above)

The Venture. An Annual of Art and Literature edited by Laurence Housman and W.Somerset Maugham
London: John Baillie
Volume 1. 1903
Contains cover design (half cloth, paper boards with design in colours on upper cover), and title page illustration (from 'The Blue Moon'), engraved by Clemence Housman, p.207, both by Housman.

The Windmill. An Illustrated Quarterly
Volume 1, No.1, October 1898
Contains a sketch, 'Marionettes' by Housman, p.60.

The Yellow Book. An Illustrated Quarterly
London: John Lane and Elkin Mathews
Volume 1, April 1894
Contains 'The Reflected Faun' pen drawing by Housman, op. p.117.
Volume 10, July 1896
Contains 'Barren Life', pen drawing by Housman.

C

LAURENCE HOUSMAN – THE CRITIC

BOOKS

Selections from the Writings of William Blake
London: Kegan Paul, Trench, Trübner & Co.
1893
With an Introductory Essay by Laurence Housman.

Arthur Boyd Houghton
London: Kegan Paul, Trench, Trübner & Co.
1896
A Selection from his work in black and white, printed for the most part from the original woodblocks. With an Introductory Essay by Laurence Housman.

The Unexpected Years by Laurence Housman
London: Cape
1937
Housman's autobiography.

MAGAZINE AND JOURNAL ARTICLES

The Album. A Journal of Photographs of Men, Women and Events of the Day
(Housman's numerous articles here appeared under 'The World of Art' or 'Our Art Supplement')
No.11; April 15, 1895; contains 'At the Royal Institute. Some observations and a Conversation' p.230.
No.12; April 22, 1895; contains 'A Note about Turner', p.272.
No.13; April 29, 1895; contains 'Some Artists at Home', p.304.
No.14; May 6, 1895; contains 'Pictures, Pictures Everywhere' (RA review), p.336.
No.15; May 13, 1895; contains 'More Pictures of the Year' (RA review) p.368.
No.18; June 3, 1895; contains 'What do you think of The Academy?', p.454.
No.21; June 24, 1895; contains 'Fair Children' (at the Grafton Galleries), p.552.
No.23; July 8, 1895; contains 'One-Man Exhibitions', pp.36-37.
No.24; July 15, 1895; contains 'You, some painters and the National Portrait Gallery', pp.68-69.
No.25; July 22, 1895; contains 'A Gossip about Subjects', pp.126-127.
No.26; July 29, 1895; contains 'On the grooves in which painters paint', pp.136-37.
No.27; August 5, 1895; contains 'The World of Art', pp.174-75.
No.28; August 12, 1895; contains 'The New Sculptor, R.A.Onslow Ford', pp.222-24.
No.37; October 14, 1895; contains 'An Art Competition-and Afterwards', pp.498-99.
No.38; October 21, 1895; contains 'Mr Baxter gives his views upon Dutch Art', p.24.
No.39; October 28, 1895; contains 'An Evening with Sir Joshua Reynolds', p.52.
No.40; November 4, 1895; contains 'A Night with Gainsborough', p.84.
No.41; November 11, 1895; contains 'Mr Baxter draws a parallel between himself and the late John Opie, R.A.', p.114.
No.42; November 18, 1895; contains 'Sir Anthony van Dyck speaks of the Martyr King', p.144.
No.43; November 25, 1895; contains 'A Midnight Colloquy about Rembrandt', p.178.
No.44; December 2, 1895; contains 'A Noble Group of Spanish Painters', p.196.

The Art Review. A Monthly Illustrated Magazine of Art, Music and Letters
Volume 1, No.1, January 1890
Contains 'Thomas Ashe', pp.143-47.

The Bibliophile. A Magazine and Review for the Collector, Student and General Reader
Volume 1, 1908
Contains 'The Illustrations of Arthur Hughes', pp. 231-37 by Housman.

Essays by Diverse Hands edited by R.W.Macan
London: Oxford University Press
New Series, Volume XII, 1933
Contains 'Pre-Raphaelitism in Art and Poetry', Housman's paper read to the Royal Society of Literature, 13 November 1929, pp.1-29.

The Magazine of Fine Arts
April 1906
Contains Housman's article, 'The Spirit of Pre-Raphaelitism', pp.406-15.

The Manchester Guardian
1895-
Housman contributed art reviews here for sixteen years.

Manchester School of Art
18 September 1911
Housman's address, 'National Art Training', delivered here.

The Studio. An Illustrated Magazine of Fine and Applied Art
Volume 31, No.134, 15 May 1904
Contains Housman's article, 'The Work of Mr Herbert Alexander', pp.301-12.

The Universal Review edited by Harry Quilter
Volume VI. 1890
Contains Housman's important article, 'Blake as an Impressionist', pp.209-22.

D
BOOK-PLATE DESIGNS BY LAURENCE HOUSMAN

The following list of book-plate designs by Housman was compiled from H.W.Fincham, *Artists and Engravers of British and American Book-plates*, 1897; Norna Labouchere, *Ladies Book-plates*, 1896; Gleeson White, "Modern Book-plates and their Designers", *The Studio*, Winter, 1898-99; Brian North Lee, *British Book-plates*, 1976; I.K.Hodgkins, *Laurence Housman Collection*, 1978; and works in the print rooms of the British Museum and Victoria and Albert Museum, London.

1 'RG', book-plate to unidentified owner (diameter 60mm).
2 'GR' (? Giles Robertson), strapwork design incorporating the initials.
3 'GR', initials disguised as the wheel of a well.
4 'Floreant Pietas et Doctrina Sancte et Sapienter', armorial design.
5 'Enjoy life while you can, Be happy while you may', vertical design of classical winged figure on a pillar, (unused design) (British Museum).
6 Robert and Evelyn Benson, pictorial design, dated 1890 (Fincham) (diameter 65mm).
7 A.W.P(ollard) pictorial design, a winged monkish scribe of strapwork, with text 'Exlibris AWP. Censurae faciendae praestitis', dated 1890 (Fincham).
8 Hannah Brace book-plate, pictorial design with two female figures.
9 S.Mathewman book-plate, pictorial design of shepherd and sheep within border.
10 Hubert Bland book-plate, pictorial design of single knight, with text 'Exlibris Huberti Bland', dated c1898 (White).
11 W.D.Weaver book-plate, pictorial design of intricate grape-vine pattern (British Museum).
12 Rose Mary Paul book-plate, floral design with

text 'Flos Brevis at Spicam' and 'Si Premis Halat Odor' (British Museum).
13 Edith Nesbit book-plate (Hodgkins, no.260).
14 'Ex Libris Fred & Emmeline Pethick Lawrence', pictorial design of robed female figure releasing a dove of 'Freedom'.

E
WOOD ENGRAVINGS BY CLEMENCE HOUSMAN

Select cuts in the *Illustrated London News* and *The Graphic* during the 1880s and early 1890s established her skill, under Charles Roberts, the noted facsimile engraver. She very occasionally signed her engravings 'C.H.sc'.

ENGRAVINGS AFTER LAURENCE HOUSMAN
The House of Joy, 1895
(re-touched process engraving)
Green Arras, 1896
The Were-Wolf, 1896
All-Fellows, 1896
The Field of Clover, 1898
Of the Imitation of Christ, 1898
The Little Land, 1899
The Blue Moon, 1904
Tennyson's *Maud*, 1905
(with Reginald Savage)
Prunella, 1907
Various bookplates (see section D)

ENGRAVINGS AFTER JAMES GUTHRIE
The Evening Star

Rossetti's *The Blessed Damozel*
Pear Tree Press
(engraved with Reginald Lodge).

Milton's *Hymn on the Morning of Christ's Nativity*
Pear Tree Press
(engraved with Reginald Lodge).

MISCELLANEOUS
Confessions of St.Augustine
London: Kegan Paul. 1900
(after Paul Woodroffe).

Of Aucassin and Nicolette
London: John Murray. 1902
(after Paul Woodroffe, translated by Laurence Housman).

The Book of Common Prayer
Essex House Press, 1903
(after C.R.Ashbee, engraved with W.H.Hooper)

Chipping Campden
Twenty-four engravings after F.L.Griggs, Oxford: Basil Blackwell, Shakespeare Head Press (printer), 1940.

INDEX